# TABLE OF CONTENTS

Foreword . . . . . . . . . . . . . . . . . . . . . . . . . . . . . . . . . . . . . . . . . iv

① The Power of Leadership . . . . . . . . . . . . . . . . . . . . . . . . . . . 1

② The Power of Vision . . . . . . . . . . . . . . . . . . . . . . . . . . . 13

③ The Power of Focusing . . . . . . . . . . . . . . . . . . . . . . . . . . . 25

④ The Power of Planning . . . . . . . . . . . . . . . . . . . . . . . . . . . 35

⑤ The Power of Effective Operations . . . . . . . . . . . . . . . . . . . . . 45

⑥ The Power of Motivation . . . . . . . . . . . . . . . . . . . . . . . . . . 59

⑦ The Power of Systems . . . . . . . . . . . . . . . . . . . . . . . . . . . 73

⑧ The Power of Getting Things Done . . . . . . . . . . . . . . . . . . . . . 81

⑨ The Power of Character . . . . . . . . . . . . . . . . . . . . . . . . . . . 95

Review: Turn on the Power . . . . . . . . . . . . . . . . . . . . . . . . . . . 105

Index . . . . . . . . . . . . . . . . . . . . . . . . . . . . . . . . . . . . . . . . 109

# FOREWORD

*Turn on the power:* Power is an enabling force to do something, or to get something done. When we turn the key on in our car we supply power to the engine enabling the car to move. The same may be true with people. Leaders influence people to act when they are able to turn on the power within people to move, do, or get things done.

People are *not* turned on and off like a light switch. People are turned on to magnify their callings by a leader who has received the spirit of his calling and leads by the power of love, positive influence, persuasion and patience. The suggestions in this book are meant to turn on the power of leaders so they can influence people with whom they work to get important things done and make a difference.

A famous professional football coach at the opening of football training season stood before his players. He said we will start with the fundamental of football. He then held up a football and said "This is a football."

In a similar manner this book is written to teach fundamentals of leadership. Hopefully to help leaders turn on the doing power in people to accomplishing planed objectives. Most leadership books are written for the professional leader, the president or CEO of a corporation. This book is written for the common ardent leader who is called to lead a group of people. A leader who wants to learn leadership principles that will turn on the power in people to achieve desired outcomes.

Presented in this book are basic leadership principles, suggestions, reminders and ideas to hopefully help leaders become more aware, more awake and more engaged in turning on the achieving power in people. These leadership principles have helped me in some of my callings to make a difference and feel the emotion of success.

The leader who applies these principles will turn on the power in himself and others and will make a difference in peoples lives and their accomplishments. He will achieve desired outcomes and feel the emotion of success. This book has not been suggested, authorized or approved by the Church or its leaders. The opinions and views expressed in this book are mine and my responsibility.

It has been my privilege to work with many different leaders in various parts of the world. In many cases the people I have worked with, when they were called to a position of leadership, may not have had the opportunity to learn some of the fundamental principles of leadership. This book is dedicated to them. It will help to answer four fundamental leadership questions:

1. **What do I want to accomplish?**
2. **What key outcomes are most important to accomplish?**
3. **How will I empower others to help me accomplish the desired outcome?**
4. **How to establish key criteria for success.**

# ACKNOWLEDGMENTS

I express heart felt thanks and gratitude for the help and many suggestions for the improvement of this book. Marilyn Lennard, Anne Mason, Peter Reynolds, Les Harris, Rodger Harris, Anthony Osborne, Ian Arden, Ronald L. Craven, Bruce Frandson.

# THE POWER OF LEADERSHIP

"God does not begin by asking us about our abilities,
but only about our availability, and if
we then prove our dependability,
he will increase our capability."
(Neal A. Maxwell, *Ensign,* July 1975, p. 7)

Think of two individuals whose leadership abilities have significantly influenced your life. What was it that created such an influence? Reflect on their leadership abilities and style. Was there something particular that they did that few others have done? As I have thought about this question, I have come to the conclusion that effective leadership is largely a matter of people influencing people in a truthful, persuasive, friendly, and purposeful manner.

Leaders are not born as leaders—each effective leader must go through a process of learning and growing. Ironically, a key ingredient in the leadership growth process is obedient "followship." Respectful obedience to a file leader and to subordinate leaders is essential to personal growth and leadership development. While attending a meeting of Church leaders with President Ezra Taft Benson, I heard him state, "When obedience becomes a quest rather than an irritant you will be endowed with power from on high."

The fundamental course for learning leadership is followship. I think of a man who was oozing with talent, ability, and the potential to become a top executive in his organization, but he failed the course in followship. He questioned most of the decisions of his file leaders. He complained about how things were done, and constantly told others how things should be done. As a result, he lost the respect of his file leaders and the opportunity to grow in the organization.

1

---

**Insight: Wise follow ship is a prerequisite to top leadership.**

---

Leadership is learned by following, receiving, and acting on directions received from a file leader. Followship is a training course in communicating, learning, and understanding how to act on counsel received. Key elements of followship are *listening, learning,* and *doing.* The degree to which we are able to follow a good leader is often the most telling indication of our own ability to lead successfully.

When called to position of leadership we often become painfully aware of our inadequacies and tend to focus on our weakness. We may be hesitant to move out of our comfort zone into a courage zone and accept new callings and responsibilities. It is important to realize that being called by prophecy also implies a promise to be given inspiration to help you magnify your calling.

Remember the words of the Lord: "If men come unto me I will show unto them their weakness. I give unto men weakness that they may be humble; and my grace is sufficient for all men that humble themselves before me; for if they humble themselves before me, and have faith in me, then will I make weak things become strong unto them" (Ether 12: 27). President Monson said it best when he said, "Whom the Lord calls, the Lord qualifies."

Effective leaders empower other people to work toward achieving desired outcomes. Significant results are accomplished when a leader and his followers honor, respect, and trust one another, thus establishing a significant level of unity. When I think about leaders who have greatly influenced my life, my thoughts focus on three important principles of leadership:

# 1. CREDIBILITY
# 2. SOCIAL ABILITY
# 3. COMMUNICATING ABILITY

# ——CREDIBILITY——

Credibility is the ability to inspire confidence—it creates in the minds and hearts of others a sense of reliability, believability, and possibility. Without credibility a leader lacks the influence to empower others because his actions speak louder than his words. People follow credibility more than they follow word ability.

A good example of credibility is a story I read about Mohandas Gandhi. A family in India had a daughter who began to eat sugar at every available opportunity. The parents could not convince her to quit. They were advised to take her to see Mohandas Gandhi. When they did, he said only, "Please come back again in two weeks." The parents were surprised by his counsel but did as he requested. When they returned Gandhi said to the girl, "Stop eating sugar." She replied, "Yes, Mohandas," and she did not have the problem again.

The parents asked Gandhi, "Why did you not give her that advice when we came two weeks ago?" In response Gandhi said, "Oh, you don't understand. You see, two weeks ago I was eating sugar." Gandhi understood the importance of creating credibility before counseling the girl. He knew he first had to walk his talk.

> **Insight: Walk your talk**

To maintain credibility and be an influential leader it is necessary for you to walk your talk. The person who has worked hard for a long time and has accumulated great wealth guards his wealth with his life. He is mindful of thieves—dishonest men and women who would take it from him if he did not care for it. So it should be with your credibility. A wise person makes sure his or her credibility is securely protected, constantly renewed, and frequently added upon. True leadership cannot exist without true credibility.

Your credibility always precedes you where ever you may go or whatever you may do. If your credibility inspires respect, creates admiration, and demonstrates competency you will have influence with other people and your responsibilities will be made easier and more successful.

You are both the major creator and the primary destroyer of your credibility. Every day of your life you are either adding to or diminishing from your credibility. Your credibility is usually first made by a single quality which brings attention to you, such as honesty, likeableness, knowledge, efficiency, or some other personal trait that gains the attention and respect of others. Your recognized abilities help create your credibility.

> **Insight: Integrity is the foundation of credibility.**

Your credibility is your character wealth. Note, however, that it must be built upon a rock-solid foundation of integrity. Integrity ensures consistency of performance based on a firm commitment to powerful values. Your credibility must be carefully guarded, built upon, and magnified by sterling qualities of moral character and earned abilities gained through self-effort, self-inspection, and self-improvement. Your credibility is an incredible power that will protect you from the unworthy, soiled, and destroying influence of others. It will set you apart from other people. It will influence other people's feelings toward you in a positive manner. It will give you power to influence other people. Clearly, your credibility enhances your leadership ability

I have hanging in my office a picture of Abraham Lincoln. He has long been a hero in my life. I have read and heard many stories about him. His character traits have made a great impression on me. As a young boy I understood him to be a person who did not smoke, chew tobacco, or drink alcohol, and who could always be trusted. Indeed, he became known as "Honest Abe." His credibility had a lot to do with his outstanding leadership ability.

When our thoughts and actions are compatible with our professed values and standards we experience inner peace and unity and become men and women of influence. When our thoughts and actions are in conflict with our professed values we often experience inner trauma and lack influence with other people. A person of integrity never has to worry about which lie he has told and to whom he has told it; thus, he is free to focus on what needs to be achieved.

The Lord outlined some basic principles of leadership credibility, along with promised blessings for faithful service, in the Doctrine and Covenants: "For whoso is faithful unto the obtaining these two priesthoods of which I have spoken, and the magnifying their calling, are sanctified by the Spirit unto the renewing of their bodies" (D&C 84:33). President Spencer W. Kimball said concerning this scripture, "Far more seems to be implied in these requirements than token obediences—far more is needed that mere attendance at a few meetings and token fulfillment of assignment. The perfection of body and spirit are implied, and that includes the kind of service that goes far beyond the normal definition of duty." [Abraham, *Example to Fathers*, p.2].

**Some basic principles of leadership are:**

1. **Be faithful in doing your duty: faith is a principle of action.**
2. **Magnify your calling: enlarge or expand your calling.**
3. **Become sanctified by the Spirit: follow the prompting of the Spirit.**
4. **Renewing your body: in the doing, you become alive concerning your calling.**

---

**Insight: A person's greatest influence is his credibility.**

---

# ———SOCIAL ABILITY———

While serving as a young officer on a ship, I was counseled by another officer not to mix with the crew. I have learned over the years that was some of the worst advice I have ever received. Sociality is a very important part of leadership. Socializing with the people he is serving gives a leader an opportunity to get to know them and builds positive and enduring relationships.

People want to be loved, needed, trusted, valued, and respected. It has been my privilege to work with men and women who were approachable, kind, well-mannered, and concerned for other people. Their positive social ability helped them create a happy, productive working environment. Such leaders have been a great influence in my life. It is a wonderful feeling to be appreciated, liked, and even loved by your leaders. You tend to work harder and care more when you know your leaders really care for you.

Social ability is a reflection of the way a leader sees and feels about himself. When a person feels comfortable and secure with himself, he builds inner confidence and positive relationships with people. Without social ability, people find it difficult to relate with openness, spontaneity, and freedom of expression and emotion. A climate of trust is essential for effective social ability.

Most of my life I have been happy in my work. However, I do remember as a young man having to work with a person who had a negative, sour, and surly disposition. I felt very uncomfortable working with him and tried to avoid him as much as possible. I did, however, learn a lot while working with him—I learned that I never wanted to be like him. I therefore determined that I would strive to be a positive person with a positive disposition and strive to eliminate the negative.

The effective leader realizes that his title is only an opportunity to prove his effectiveness. He has to create positive and supportive relationships and cooperative associations with people. He must inspire, motivate, direct, and guide. He has to learn how to relate and unite, then to achieve results. He at times must reach beyond his felt abilities to influence others to do not only their best but whatever is necessary.

Your success or failure to a great degree depends on your mental attitude. Your thoughts about yourself and other people. The way you look, and carry yourself, the way you walk, talk and behave. The first indication of a effectual attitude is your smile. Your smile tells a lot about your inner self. Social ability includes building friendships by being approachable.

While visiting with a man I asked him, "What do you do in your ward?" He told me he was the bishop, and he ran the ward. I found out in his case that was a true statement. He not only ran the ward, he also ran the people in the ward. He forgot that people make things happen in a ward. His leadership skills lacked social ability, and his heart lacked spirituality. The ward seemed stagnant, lifeless, and colorless.

> **Insight: Social ability is the result of love, trust, and faith in people.**

## ———COMMUNICATING ABILITY———

As a young man I reported to a leader who had very limited communication skills. In my discussions with him, his answers to me were not clear. He made comments like this: " I guess so." "Oh, usually." "You should know how to do that." "I don't have time right now." "Maybe." I often did not know what he was thinking or what he expected of me. I felt his communications skills were unclear and shallow. I was pleased when circumstances caused me to report to a different leader.

Years later I reported to a person whose talk seemed never ending. He carried his conversation to the extreme. He talked to the subject, over it, under it, through it, and around it, which caused me to become uptight from listening to a lot of unnecessary conversation.

Fortunately, most of the leaders with whom I have worked were leaders whose language was precise and meaningful (giving both information and direction), who could defuse potential problems with humor and positive comments, and who could direct people's energy and thinking to accomplish specific results.

> **Insight: Effective communications involves influencing people to do what is required.**

I have found over the years that one of the most challenging leadership styles to work with is the defensive leader, the leader who continually defends his point of view or ideas against the suggestions of others. Inflexibility to the thoughts and ideas of others turns them off and impedes progress.

**A defensive leader:**

**1. Causes limited and cautious discussion.**
**2. Listens with judgment rather than understanding.**
**3. Stifles counsel from others.**
**4. Stops progress.**

The non-defensive leader is usually respected and radiates the spirit of his calling—and therefore becomes more confident in his leadership ability. He is also more sure concerning decisions he makes because he has listened to other viewpoints and is making decisions based on wise counsel. Most important, the non-defensive leader usually has the Spirit to help him interpret the feelings of the people he works with and therefore has the inspired ability to sense what is going on in their hearts and minds. The non-defensive leader receives better and more crucial information. He listens and hears other people and receives suggestions that give him important and timely information.

> **Insight: The non-defensive leader listens, ponders, and learns from the suggestions of others.**

One of the greatest communication skills is the ability to listen, understand, and thereby obtain the right information to make right decisions. The effective communicator has the ability of turning even casual conversation into result-achieving conversation. Effective leaders listen, think, and take time to organize their thinking and conversation to enlighten, persuade, and create understanding.

I have worked with people who made it difficult to know what they wanted because they talked in mixed objectives. For example, let's assume you were going to Brother and Sister Smith's home for a social activity at 7:00 P.M. You found the street where they live but you do not know exactly which home is theirs, so you stop a passerby to ask for direction. Following are two ways you could ask for the help you need:

Mixed objective: "Pardon me, but we are invited to Jack Smith's home. He and his wife are holding a social activity at 7:00 P.M. I'm confident that their home is on this street, but we are not sure which is their home. Could you tell me which home belongs to the Smiths?

Specific objective: "Pardon me, the Smiths live on this street—could you please tell me which is their home?

Remember, your objective is to find the right home, not to inform some person whom you have never before met about your social calendar. To overcome communicating mixed objectives, learn to first think clearly by asking yourself key questions:

**1. What do I want to achieve?**
**2. What is my purpose?**
**3. What information must I share in order to get the answer I need?**
**4. What information is extraneous and should not be mentioned?**

A good communicator is approachable, knows what he wants, and creates a climate for achieving it.

When you have a specific objective to achieve and need the help of others, communicate in specific, clear sentences. By contrast, when in casual conversation it may be appropriate to talk in paragraphs. Seldom talk in chapters. In any case, the important objective is to communicate so people do not misunderstand.

After you have asked people to do something, it is important to let them do it. Often their way may not be the way you would do it yourself. That's okay: it's important to keep the end in mind, rather than the process. To be overly anxious about how something is done rather than simply focusing on the fact that it needs to be done often uses a lot of emotional energy on the part of both the leader and those he is anxiously pushing to get the task done. As a result, people may resent being pushed and do just enough to get by or to get the task over with.

To focus on achieving results in an important part of effective leadership. The leader who does not expect results from those he leads will never effectively lead. Further, he who does not follow up on assignments will never effectively lead. At times following up necessitates tender boldness, being kind but firm in your request. I have found that nonjudgmental questions are often more effective than demands or commands. Questions stir the mind and heart to think and ponder. People are more willing to respond to a question than a command. Teachers know that students learn by responding to questions. Effective leaders are effective teachers who cause people to think and do.

Understanding people's attitudes, concerns, and desires is necessary to teach and to lead. You can improve people's credibility, social ability, and communicating ability more effectively by asking them questions rather than by lecturing to them.

**Ponder the following questions that you might ask those whom you lead:**

1. **What are we doing very well?**
2. **What are we doing that can be improved?**
3. **What problems are you experiencing?**
4. **What is bothering you that we can talk about?**
5. **What do you see are the greatest obstacles in performing your responsibilities?**
6. **What can I do to make your work more satisfying?**

In striving to improve your leadership skills, strive to improve your credibility, social ability, and communicating ability, then you will also improve your leadership ability. These three qualities influence relationships positively and create the power that moves people and organizations to success.

He who gains a victory over other men is strong;
But he who gains a victory over himself is powerful.
— Lao-Tse

> **Insight: Understanding is the key to learning, improving, and leading.**

Strive to (1) strengthen your credibility, (2) increase your social ability, and (3) improve your communicating ability, and you will turn on the power in your organization.

# THE POWER OF LEADERSHIP

| Credibility | Ok | Need to Improve |
|---|:---:|:---:|
| 1. I am serving and leading by example. | ✓ | |
| 2. I feel the love and support of all the people with whom I work. | | ✓ |
| 3. I work at creating credibility. | ✓ | |
| 4. People understand my expectations of them. | | ✓ |
| 5. Each person is doing what is necessary and expected. | | ✓ |

## Social Ability

| | Ok | Need to Improve |
|---|:---:|:---:|
| 1. People feel my friendliness, warmth, and openness. | ✓ | |
| 2. I am fair and reasonable. I am not the judge and jury. | ✓ | |
| 3. I work at showing caring and concern for others. | ✓ | |
| 4. I give many compliments and express praise often. | | ✓ |
| 5. I am helping others to grow. | ✓ | |

*through my example*

## Communication Ability

| | Ok | Need to Improve |
|---|:---:|:---:|
| 1. I create a freedom of communication. | | ✓ |
| 2 I try to communicate clearly and specifically. | | ✓ |
| 3. My language is concise and meaningful. | ✓ | |
| 4. I am a good listener. | ✓ | |
| 5. I am effective in communicating results rather than activities. | ✓ | |

# THE POWER OF VISION

"The first basic ingredient of leadership is a guiding vision."
Warren Bennis, *Becoming a Leader,* p.19

An excited young man drove into his driveway, sprang from his car, and ran into his house. Barely had he opened the door before he began shouting, "Mom, I'm in love! I have met the most wonderful girl. She is everything I ever wanted." Mom of course immediately asked, "Who is this girl? Tell me about her. Where did you meet her? Who are her parents?" The young man then unveiled to his mother his feelings about his girlfriend. He told his mother all about his girlfriend with passion and enthusiasm. The young man had a vision, and he shared it in such a way that his mother soon began to share in that vision.

Just as this young man had a vision, so must the effective leader. His personal vision of his calling is important in setting the direction and character of the organization. He determines his vision when he decides what he wants to do and to be remembered for in his calling. His personal vision precedes the vision of the organization.

For some time now I have been fascinated by how the Lord prepared Moses for his calling. The Lord first and foremost had His own personal vision that He shared with Moses: "This is my work and my glory—to bring to pass the immortality and eternal life of man" (Moses 1:39). The Lord called His servant by name and said, essentially, "I have a work for thee, Moses, my son." Moses was then called to free and save Israel. Significantly, as Moses filled his calling, he also helped the Lord to accomplish His greater vision of bringing "to pass the immorality and eternal life of man."

The first chapter of Moses gives us a good understanding of the importance of a leadership vision when calling men and women to help accomplish the Lord's work. Consider these steps:

1. **The Lord called Moses (Articles of Faith 1:5).**
2. **The Lord gave Moses a vision concerning his calling (Moses 1:6–39).**
3. **The Lord communicated the end result he wanted Moses to achieve (Moses 1:39).**
4. **The Lord listened to Moses' questions to create understanding (Moses 1:30 –37).**
5. **The Lord taught and inspired Moses with the faith to achieve his calling (Moses 2–8).**

An organizational vision is the dream of a leader and his followers. A compelling vision causes the leader to "see" and "feel" what needs to be done in the future. Many leaders are so involved in the here and now that they neglect their responsibility to look ahead for future opportunities. The shared vision of the leader and his followers becomes the motivational energy behind every effort and the force that guides and pushes those involved in the work through problems, difficulties, and challenges as they work to achieve the vision..

I have observed that great leaders in my life have had two things in common: One, they knew where they were going. Two, they had the leadership ability to persuade others to go with them.

Determining your vision is like planning a trip. First, you determine the desired outcome you want from your trip; then you must decide how to get there. The vision is the drawing and motivating power to get there.

> **Insight : When a leader is motivated by a desired vision, he is not easily discouraged, dissuaded, or defeated.**

Peter Drucker, author of many books on management, said: "The answer to the question, what is our business? is the first responsibility of top management" (*Management, Tasks, Responsibilities, Practices,* p. 73).

While attending a seminar for new temple presidents, the manager of one of the temple departments made a statement that caused me to know that President Hinckley has a vision of Church work. The manager said, "When we prepare a presentation to be reviewed by President Hinckley, we know that we must always answer three questions during the presentation.

1. **Will it bring more baptismal converts into the church?**
2. **Will it reconvert the less active?**
3. **Will it fill the temples?**

He continued, "If our proposal hasn't answered those three questions appropriately, it hasn't a chance of getting approved by President Hinckley.

The power of purpose—often written in the form of a vision or mission statement—helps you to judge all your activities, programs, and events against the purpose of the organization. You just have to ask the question: "Does what you are proposing help to accomplish the purpose and achieve the vision of the organization?" If it does, consider its implementation; if it does not, then modify it or discard it

Know what you want to achieve, then pay the price to achieve it this is the path to greatness. "Purpose" accompanied with a shared "vision" gives a leader and his followers a strong sense of direction and commitment to:

> See it!
> Desire it!
> Achieve it!

---

**Insight: If you do not know where you are going, you can be sure that the people in the organization will follow you.**

---

The call to leadership is a call to influence the future. Many leaders are too busy with less important things to envision future opportunities. To create a compelling vision that will make a difference in your organization, consider doing the following:

Ask yourself "Do I have Time for This"?

15

# 1. PERFORM A CRITICAL ANALYSIS
# 2. SET DIRECTION / *Goals.*
# 3. COMMUNICATE EXPECTATIONS

## ———PERFORM A CRITICAL ANALYSIS———

When going into a big shopping center for the first time, I usually first look for a building map or directory. Standing in front of the building directory, I determine first where I am and then determine how to get to where I want to go. In essence, I first perform a critical analysis of my new environment, starting with where I am now so I can see where I want to go. Similarly, you should perform critical analysis of your organization in order to determine how you are doing now and what you need to do to achieve your desired major objectives, which in turn lead to accomplishing your vision.

### POSSIBILITIES AND OPPORTUNITIES

Every organization has its problems, challenges, and opportunities. Organizational analysis can pinpoint areas of need, fix or modify existing conditions, and give new and compelling direction to the future. Opportunities come when we overcome the problems and accept the challenges. The innovative and resourceful leader identifies the possibilities and maximizes the opportunities.

While serving as a regional representative, I had the privilege of working with a stake president who made a critical analysis of his stake organization at the end of each year. He wanted to determine whether some activities and programs should be terminated and what were some future possibilities for achieving new results and creating more opportunities. He realized that activities and programs that do not produce desired outcomes were simply excess fat in the organization, void of muscle and causing excess busy work that did not produce desired result. Through his analysis he was able to determine the success of inspired programs of the Church and also locate the activity fat that had collected around those programs.

During November or December each year he held an analysis meeting with his stake leadership council to prepare for the new year. The purpose of the meeting was to determine which activities and programs were largely fat and should be trimmed down or done away with. The stake leadership council was also challenged to seek new opportunities for the coming year in the form of new objectives or outcomes that were in harmony with the mission of the Church. He realized that continually doing the same things the same way creates the same results. His yearly analysis (which could also have been every six months) breathed new life and anticipation into the people in his organization. He would think! In order to get the members of the stake council to think as well, he would not ask closed questions that could be answered yes or no or even with a simple statement. He asked open questions that caused the people to think, and he stimulated discussion so he could determine feelings and attitudes. He asked such questions as:

**1. What is your purpose as a leader in this stake?**
**2. In what ways do you feel we are progressing?.**
**3. In what ways do you feel we are not progressing?**

After these special council meetings were held, ideas and suggestions were prioritized in order of the most important opportunities that would help to accomplish the purpose and vision of the stake. To implement these new opportunities, he assigned the most productive members of the leadership council to lead out in taking advantage of these opportunities. Those leaders in turn set the proper example for the less-productive members of the council.

His philosophy was to empower his leadership team with greater desire and ability to contribute and achieve the purpose and vision of the organization. He worked hard to overcome lethargic attitudes of just putting in time, of just doing but not achieving. He was result directed. He expected people to contribute in the form of completed results.

Throughout the year **he continually asks himself and others fact-finding questions:**

1. **In what areas are we improving?**
2. **In what areas do we need to improve?**
3. **How can we improve?**

These questions helped him to become more aware of what was happening in the stake and to determine the strengths, weaknesses, and future opportunities within the stake.

---

**Insights: A compelling vision creates the future.**

---

The process that this stake president went through was not complicated. It required no extensive training. But it was effective, in part because he was consistent in applying it, month in and month out. In short, he:

1. *Studied* the statistics and determined the vital signs by talking with people.
2. *Determined* what had happened, what was happening, and what he wanted to happen.
3. *Identified* concerns, problems, challenges, and opportunities.
4. *Prioritized* the information gathered.
5. *Created* a revised and compelling vision that would teach, reach, and achieve.

Your vision, if appealing and used, will be something you will live, walk, eat, and sleep. It will be a daily motivating power in your life and work. It will help you and others overcome mediocrity and cause everyone concerned to focus on right outcomes. People who are involved in creating the vision of the organization are also motivated to help accomplish the vision. Shared vision gives people the opportunity to think, ponder, participate, and grow. The vision then becomes more important than their own personal concerns.

---

**Insight: Walking and talking your vision brings expected results.**

---

## ———SET DIRECTION———

With information gained from a critical analysis of your organization and after talking to people in that organization, take a pencil and paper or a keyboard and revise your vision statement with challenging, motivating, and action-compelling possibilities. Meet with your leadership team and create a shared vision statement that sets the direction for the people in the organization. This will be a vision of new opportunities. Remember that creating a motivating vision takes time and mental exertion. Be willing to pay the price, to take the necessary time to ponder and think of the best thing to do that will improve people performance and bring organizational success. Often some leaders are so busy that they do not make time to think, analyze, and plan, and they therefore do not receive inspiration regarding new ideas and new direction. Focus your vision on those areas that will have the greatest benefit on achieving the purpose of the organization.

---

**Insight: Where emphasis is focused, results will be.**

---

When an accident victim is wheeled into the emergency room of a hospital and is lying on the examining table showing the effects of a very serious accident, the doctor is first concerned about the person's breathing, head, heart, and pulse rather than any cuts and bruises; he understands that the head, heart, and pulse signal the important vital signs for maintaining life in the body. Once the core bodily functions are taken care of, the doctor can move down the priority list to other areas of potential concern.

When setting organizational direction, be mindful of those areas that will have the greatest impact on accomplishing the purpose of the organization and the mission of the Church. Be mindful also of the most important vital signs expressed by people, determine conditions and focus on the opportunities that will achieve the purpose and vision of your organization. Modify, sharpen, and invigorate your vision in order to keep it alive in the minds and hearts of those whom you lead. Help them to—

**See it!**
**Want it!**
**Reach it!**

**Insight: What you see, feel, desire, and act upon, you get.**

A vision statement that is challenging, realistic, and accompanied with measurable expectations sets the direction of the organization.

**Your shared vision statement should:**

1. **Have value in the lives of the people.**
2. **Influence behavior to positive action.**
3. **Cause people to think and ponder.**
4. **Build commitment in the minds and hearts of the people.**
5. **Encourage people and organizational growth.**

A motivating vision statement not only sets direction but also builds excitement, expectation, and a willingness to follow. It helps to overcome mediocrity and causes people to focus on important objectives. The vision statement must be a shared vision. People who are involved in creating the vision of the organization are also motivated to help accomplish the vision.

The German poet Goethe said: "The greatest genius will not be worth much if he pretends to draw exclusively from his own resources."

# ————COMMUNICATE EXPECTATIONS————

One summer we created great excitement in our children to fulfill certain tasks at home. Now, our children were no different than most. Domestic chores and duties did not rank high on their priority list. But this summer they understood that if they would perform these tasks, as a family we would go to Disneyland. They had a vision, and they knew our expectations. Regular follow-up reminders during family home evening kept alive their excitement to complete our expectations so we could go to Disneyland . Needless to say, it was a productive summer and a great experience for the family!

When leaders clearly present expectations in a spirit of love and appreciation, they create positive acceptance and desired movement. People then move forward, believing and achieving the expectations, and are most likely to be happy in their callings

Effective leaders understand that obtaining positive acceptance of any presentation takes pondering time and some preparation. The presentation of expectations will have a good chance of receiving a favorable response:

**If your presentation:**

1. **Shows sincere interest in the people who will achieve your expectations;**
2. **Is interesting and open to the comments and suggestions of the people; and**
3. **Your expectations are clear, realistic, acceptable, and attainable;**
4. **Your expectations are in harmony with the mission of the Church.**

When calling people to positions of responsibility, make sure that you clearly explain your expectations of them in order to create in their mind a vision of what they are to accomplish. Without vision and clear expectations people and organizations can atrophy and stagnate.

Perhaps the most neglected of all leadership processes is formulating a compelling organizational vision and the accompanying planned expectations that you and the people in your organization desire, see, believe, and can achieve.

People can get excited to accomplish expected objectives when they see the gulf between current organizational reality and the possibilities and value of achieving future objectives. However, the future objectives must be more important to the people than current reality if they are to be motivated to achieve those objectives. When people feel that they are needed and individually can help make a difference, they will be supportive, cooperative, and achievement-oriented.

When you present your expectations to the people in your organization, you will need three basic ingredients in your formula for success:

**1. Up-to-date information concerning current reality.**
**2. A clear picture of future results to be achieved .**
**3. An understanding of the benefits to be gained from achieving the results.**

> **Insight: The best way to predict the future is to create it.**

Any one of these ingredients without the others will do very little to bring about the new and desired outcomes.

Helping people understand current reality alone does not create the excitement to achieve future objectives. People will not be discontent with current reality, nor will they seek to achieve future objectives— unless they see a new vision for change and understand the benefits that will come from performing new standards of performance.

William James said, "Need and struggle are what excite and inspire us." People are inspired when they are asked to do something they know is of value. Sustained action is born out of a vision that requires dedication and commitment as opposed to wishing, day dreaming, and just talking. One of the enemies of progress is fuzzy thinking and unclear expectations concerning future objectives to be achieved. Clear expectations and direction are necessary to create and accomplish a compelling vision.

---

**INSIGHT: WITHOUT VISION AND DIRECTION, SUBORDINATE LEADERS LEAD.**

---

(Vision is a product of mental execution.) When a leader focuses his mind on organizational improvements, individual growth, and achieving desired results, his mind is enlightened by the power of the Holy Spirit. Keep in mind Joseph Smith's statement, "There is a superior intelligence bestowed upon such as obey the Gospel with full purpose of heart" (*Teachings of the Prophet Joseph Smith,* p.67). Vision is a product of diligent prayer and an inquiring mind. It comes to the mind in the form of ideas, suggestions, and inner promptings to do something, to act according to the inspiration received. We are reminded in Proverbs: "Where there is no vision, the people perish" (Proverbs 29:18).

## GIVE PEOPLE A VISION OF WHAT THEY CAN DO AND BECOME

Determine the purpose of your organization. Create a compelling vision. 1. Perform a critical analysis, 2. set direction, 3. communicate expectations in the form of desired results, and you will turn on the achieving power in your organization.

# THE POWER OF VISION

## THE PURPOSE OF OUR ORGANIZATION IS

_____

_____

_____

## PONDER YOUR VISION STATEMENT

1. What do you feel those above you in the organization want you to achieve?
2. What do you feel is most important for your organization to achieve?
3. What is your inspired and desired outcome?
4. List three grand wishes you would want your organization to achieve.

## WRITE YOUR VISION STATEMENT

_____

_____

_____

_____

_____

_____

_____

_____

_____

_____

# THE POWER OF FOCUSING

The price is first of all singleness of purpose
and concentration of effort
(W. R. Gresham, *Nothing Is Impossible,* p. 53).

When I was a young man I went on a Boy Scout camping trip. We had to make a fire without the use of matches. Fortunately, I had planned ahead—in my camp gear I had a little magnifying glass. We put some small kindling on top of a piece of paper. Then I took the magnifying glass and focused the sun's rays though the magnifying glass onto the piece of paper.

The magnified light from the sun rays created heat energy on the surface of the paper and caused the paper to catch fire. This in turn started the kindling, and by carefully watching the flame we soon had a big fire without using matches. By focusing the energy of the sun rays onto the paper, a fire was created.

When it comes to Church callings, focusing is the ability to direct leadership and organizational energy to achieve important objectives and results. When a leader determines the most important objectives to be accomplished and focuses all the available energy on achieving the results that will in turn accomplish those objectives, success will be achieved. Focusing concentrates the collective energy of the minds and hearts of the members of the leadership council to achieve specific desired outcomes. These concentrated energies result in igniting the fire of achievement.

Without focused direction some leaders spend their time managing activities rather than accomplishing results. Focused leaders are usually results-oriented leaders. They realize that accomplishing results is what moves organizations forward and helps their people to gain the skills they need. They do not get carried away in promoting activities, programs, and events unless they produce the desired results. They realize that programs, activities, and events should be the means of achieving the end results, not take the place of those results.

Successful achievement comes with the ability to envision the future, to dream a dream, to see in advance the results and a deadline for achieving those results. Achieving leaders will:

## 1. FOCUS ON ACHIEVING RESULTS
## 2. FOCUS ON SUSTAINED ATTENTION
## 3. FOCUS ON PURPOSEFUL ACTION

## ———FOCUS ON ACHIEVING RESULTS———

We can probably safely assume that most important objectives are established so they can be achieved. Why else establish an objective? Effective leaders, knowing that their organizations will seek to achieve their objectives, will explain *why* each objective is so important. They will ensure that people understand *what* is to be achieved and *how* they are to achieve it. Such an understanding crystallizes thinking into motivating knowledge that focuses on achieving the right results in the right way.

If a leader does not know *what* he wants to accomplish, does not understand *why* it is important to accomplish a particular result, nor has any idea of *how* to accomplish it, any road will get him to where he is going. Knowledge, understanding, and doing create the power to influence others to achieve end results and desired objectives.

> **Insight: Focusing on important results inspires and empowers people to action.**

When you feel you have identified the most important results to be achieved and believe you can achieve them, your belief and focusing power will cause you to generate the necessary energy to overcome any negative, passive, or otherwise resistive force. You will light the fire of achievement under those who are then assigned to accomplish the results and planned objectives.

**Think, write, and communicate:**

1. **What are the most important major objectives?**
2. **What is the most important result needed to accomplish each objective?**
3. **Why are these objectives and results so important?**
4. **How can I inspire others to achieve these results?**

---

**Insight: Great leaders are average leaders who are focused.**

---

It is very important to remember that the status quo is at best maintained when there is no focused direction. Without direction, an organization exists in the past. Unless a leader's expectations and performance does not change, the organization's performance will not change.

While attending a leadership training meeting, I listened to a discussion between an effective stake president and those attending the meeting. One of the individuals addressed the president with a comment that he had tried to accomplish a certain task but had not been successful. He asked the president what he should do. I was impressed with this good leader's response. He first asked, "What is your objective?" After listening to the response, the president said, "Your objective is right. Therefore you should change your focus. Make it a matter of prayer. Think and ponder on several different approaches to achieve your objective." He did not take responsibility to solve the problem. He did, however, cause the individual to rethink and focus on some new and different approaches to achieve his objectives. He recognized that the objective was good, and the individual seemed to understand why it should be sought, but the problem lie with the *how* of accomplishing. In other words, the president helped the individual understand the process for solving his problem without removing his responsibility for solving it.

---

**Insight: Where your focus goes, so flows your energy.**

---

**When you focus on achieving desired results, you:**

**1. Set the direction for individuals to achieve specific results.**
**2. Direct and guide people's mental and physical energy.**
**3. Achieve future opportunities.**
**4. Guide people in making quality decisions.**
**5. Give people satisfaction from successful achievement.**

The leader who establishes measurable results and sets standards of performance will receive the reward. By contrast, the leader who thinks and manages in generalities will only achieve generalities. When specific results are determined, delegated, and accepted, along with the establishment of clear and measurable standards of performance, results will be achieved.

---

**Insight: What gets measured, gets done.**

---

**1. *Focus* on what you want to achieve.**
**2. *Prioritize* what you want to focus on.**
**3. *Achieve* what you focus on.**

## ——FOCUS ON SUSTAINED ATTENTION——

William James stated, "Genius is nothing but a power of sustained attention" (*Psychology Briefer Course,* p.101).

If expected results lack interest and emotional appeal, attention will be diverted into doing that which people feel like doing (usually something interesting and emotionally appealing!) rather than what they are expected to do. When attention is divided, motivation suffers and results are not achieved.

A reservoir can flow leisurely into a river that descends down through a valley. It can also be channeled and focused through three or four openings that turn turbines and produce the energy that provides electricity for all the people in the valley. Some leaders leisurely flow down the valley of mediocrity carried by the currents of the organization. Other leaders pay attention to the organizational flow and see that it is channeled and focused in the right direction in order to achieve the desired outcome. Leaders succeed in proportion to the weakness or strength of their attention to achieving desired results.

> **Insight: Explain, not just tell, what you expect to be achieved.**

**When expecting to get things done through other people:**

**1. Making decisions may not be enough.**
**2. Determining results may not be enough.**
**3. Telling people what to do may not be enough.**
**4. Delegating end results to a specific person with a specific date may be enough.**

More productive leaders focus on spending about 3/4 of their time thinking and organizing specifics of people improvement, performance improvement, and achieving improvement. They spend about 1/4 of their time doing administrative and paper work.

If allowed, administrative work can take up most of a leader's time. Attention should be directed to doing, achieving, and improving work, which necessitates controlling the tendency for shallow talking, one-on-one debating, and unproductive discussions. However, balance is necessary. Keep in mind that too much command and control stifles motivation. It is most important to be sensitive to people's feelings and needs. Unhappy people are usually not productive people.

**Sustained attention to achieve important results has power to:**

**1. Eliminate pressure because it discourages nonessential activities.**
**2. Overcome people working at cross-purposes with each other.**
**3. Overcome conflicting opinions in getting agreed upon things done.**

Paying attention to achieving key results is to make sure that the most important matters are not squeezed out by less important matters.

**Think**: Does this activity contribute to what needs to be accomplished?

---

**Insight: We achieve what we focus on.**

---

**Focused leaders pay attention to:**

**1. Keeping the leadership team alert and focused.**
**2. Helping people achieve important results.**
**3. Helping people grow, learn, improve, and achieve.**

"What holds attention determines action"
(William James, *Psychology Briefer Course,* p. 443).

## ———FOCUS ON PURPOSEFUL ACTION———

Action guided by a purpose has achieving power. The Prophet Joseph Smith stated that "[it] is faith, and faith only, which is the moving cause of all action" (*Lectures on Faith,* p. 2). **Faith is a principle of action.** It is the motivating power to get things done. The Lord indicated that we should not have to be commanded in all things. Rather we should be anxiously engaged in a good cause (see D&C 58:26 –27).

**Three keys to taking action are:**

**1. Take action to do that which is pressing on your mind.**
**2. Think and identify the benefits for taking action.**
**3. Start now, or commit to a time to start.**

I have found these three principles helpful in taking action. That is why I strive to get my home teaching done the first of the month. It relieves my mind of the pressing duty to get my home teaching done. It blesses the families we visit with a message from the First Presidency. It gives me a feeling of faith and accomplishment.

---

**Insight: Purposeful and dominant thoughts
are determiners of action.**

---

Albert Einstein said, "The significant problems we face cannot be solved at the same level of thinking we were at when we created them."

When purposeful ideas and expected results are presented on a higher level of thinking than previously communicated, and are presented in a different, interesting and creative manner the ideas will usually be accepted. People will focus on and accept ideas that have a purpose and are:

**NEW - EXCITING - DIFFERENT
BENEFICIAL - ACHIEVABLE**

Ho hum casual conversations, presentations, and delegated assignments never stir people to action. Effective leaders think the careful way rather than the casual way. It takes inspired conversation to do new things in a new and purposeful manner. One of the most powerful practices you can learn is the power of purposeful thinking and doing.

**Purposeful thinking causes:**

**1. Dreams to be accomplished.**
**2. People's energy focused and directed.**
**3. People to make a difference.**

Purposeful thinking and action are necessary to direct people's thoughts, energy, and resources to achieve the desired outcomes of the leaders. Focusing on achieving a right purpose is a necessary to achieve desired outcomes.

During a training meeting with a group of bishops I observed a counselor in a stake presidency focus on *why* something was not done rather than focusing on what the person or persons did not do. He focused on the problem rather than the individuals. When he asked why planned results were not accomplished he got superficial answers. He did not stop after the first superficial answer but continued to ask why. Eventually he received a lot of good feedback information. He and the bishops understood better why expected actions were not done, and they were then able to focus on new approaches.

Leaders are often so eager to get a job done that they continually push individuals to achieve the results they want. Sometimes they should first ask why isn't the job done and find out the reasons for lack of accomplishment.

**Asking why planned results were not accomplished creates the following conditions:**

**1. Determines a reason for lack of productivity from those who should produce.**
**2. Gets people involved in finding the answers to non-productive conditions.**
**3. Gives the file leader the opportunity to make corrective suggestions.**
**4. Motivates people to be more effective in producing what needs to be done.**

When you select the most important objectives to focus on, you can then better judge your time and use your abilities to more effectively accomplish what truly needs to be done. You will realize that as long as you are focusing on those few things that matter most, you will feel less stress and things will be achieved in the right order. Organizations prosper, linger, or die as a result of a leader's ability or inability to breathe life and purpose into the lives of the people and inspire them to believe and achieve that which is most important. A leader gives purpose to peoples work when he focuses on:

1. **Perfecting performance**
2. **Future opportunities**
3. **Solving problems**
4. **Making a difference**
5. **Achieving results**
6. **Giving life and energy to the organization**

**Focus on (1) achieving end results while maintaining, (2) sustained attention and, (3) directing your efforts to purposeful action, and you will turn on the power in your organization.**

# THE POWER OF FOCUSING

**Brainstorm: What are the most important objectives to focus on:**

1. _____    6. _____
2. _____    7. _____
3. _____    8. _____
4. _____    9. _____
5. _____    10. _____

**From the list above, select what you feel are the three most important objectives to focus on:**

1. _____
2. _____
3. _____

**List specific results in order to achieve those three important objectives.**

1. _____
2. _____
3. _____

# THE POWER OF PLANNING

"The single biggest weakness of most leaders...
they spend too much time doing and not enough
time thinking about what they are doing."
(Lin Bothwell, *The Art of Leadership*)


As a young man during World War II, I had the experience of working on a number of ships and going to different parts of the world. I never knew of a single ship's captain who went out into the open sea without a specific destination in mind and without having a detailed plan for getting there. He knew that without such a plan he would be under the influence of waves, wind, currents, and other circumstances that would dictate the direction of his ship. In short, the ship would soon be out of his control.

Too often some leaders, because they either fail to plan or do so poorly, allow themselves to be influenced by the winds of circumstances, the currents of organizational pressures, and the waves of other people's desires as they lead the organization onto an uncharted course. Just as a ship's captain before going to sea does the planning necessary to ensure success in his ultimate objective, effective leaders realize that much of an organization's success or failure is determined in the planning room, long before the first action is officially taken.

## Why plan?

1. **You will become a pro-active leader rather than reactive.**
2. **You will become a problem solver.**
3. **You will be able to do more in less time.**
4. **You will become a better organized leader.**
5. **You will have greater influence on the behavior of others.**
6. **You will be a more successful leader.**

While visiting with a bishop who was having some challenges in his ward, I asked him what his major responsibility was as the bishop? He said, "Running the ward." I asked him where he was running it to. He looked at me and asked, "What do you mean?" We discussed the need for planning in order to determine the future of the ward. As we talked he admitted that he was so busy doing busy work that he did not make time to plan or think about the future of his ward.

Effective leaders involve themselves in:

# 1. PLANNING FUTURE DIRECTION.
# 2. PLANNING IMPORTANT OBJECTIVES.
# 3. PLANNING FOR SUCCESS.

## ———PLANNING FUTURE DIRECTION———

To make a difference requires planning. A plan is a blueprint for accomplishing a desired outcome. Planning should indicate how to get from where you are now to where you want to go. Planning provides the detail of how to get there and how to do it effectively. Planning is organizing the areas of focus in order to accomplish desired pre-determined outcome.

> **Insight: First determine the desired outcome,
> then plan how to achieve it.**

Proper planning leads to determining direction and establishing major objectives. There are two important kinds of planning: strategic planning and operational planning.

**Strategic planning** starts with the thinking and pondering of the key leader at the top. Strategic planning must also include other key leaders because strategic planning involves thinking, deciding, and focusing on the present and future achievements. Every leader should become a strategic thinker. When there is united effort in strategic planning, that effort provides direction, clarifies what is expected, and guides the momentum to achieve the objectives of the organization. Effective leaders plan future outcomes.

Strategic planning takes mental exertion plus faith It is hard work, which is why most leaders do not do it. Strategic planning requires creative and innovative thinking and visualizing the desired outcome. Many leaders end up in crisis management because they have not done sufficient strategic planning..

**Strategic planning:**

**1. Determine the major objectives of the organization.**
**2. Considers the organization's strengths and weakness.**
**3. Determine new methods, new approaches, and new opportunities.**
**4. Determines possible hazards, opposition, attitudes, failure points.**
**5. Creates motivation for achievement.**

There is a commonly used strategic planning method called **SWOT** that can be used to analyze key areas in an organization:

**S**TRENGTHS

**W**EAKNESSES

**O**PPORTUNITIES

**T**HREATS

**SWOT** can be your formula for strategic planning.

**Operational planning** involves the way that the various groups or units within an organization do their work. Key leaders of these groups must first understand the strategic plan of the organization. The key unit leaders should be prepared and encouraged to plan specific goals to accomplish the major objectives. The simplest form of operational planning is first to know the major objectives derived from strategic planning and why those objectives are important, and then do what is necessary to achieve the objectives.

**Determine:**

1. **Where we are now?**
2. **Where do we want to be?**
3 **How are we are going to get there?**
4. **Who is responsible to get us there?**
5. **When should we arrive there?**

---

**Insight: Good plans produces good results.**

---

President Ezra Taft Benson gave the following good counsel concerning planning:

> "Usually the Lord gives us the overall objectives to be accomplished and some guidelines to follow, but he expects us to work out most of the details and methods. The methods and procedures are usually developed through study and prayer and by living so that we obtain and follow the prompting of the Spirit. Less spiritually advanced people, such as those in the days of Moses, had to be commanded in many things. Today those spiritually alert can look at the objective, check the guidelines laid down by the Lord and his prophets, and then prayerfully act—without having to be commanded 'in all things.' This attitude prepares men for godhood" (Conference Report, April 1965, p. 121).

Planning is never really finished. A plan is a representation of the present view of what must be done in order to accomplish the purpose, vision, and objectives of the organization. Planning continues as long as leaders keep asking the question, "How are we doing?" Planning is a prerequisite to analyzing key trends, problems, achievements, attitudes, and feelings relative to the progress of the organization or group.

> **Insight: A leader without a plan is a drifter**.

## ———PLANNING IMPORTANT OBJECTIVES———

There has been considerable discussion concerning objectives and goals. The best explanation I have read on this subject was made by Malcolm W. Pennington, past president of the Marketing Planning Group, Inc.:

A reasonable consistent distinction is developing between the meaning of the words 'objectives' and 'goals.' Objectives can best be described as the broad general aims of the organization, essentially a 'wish list.' Goals, on the other hand, are specific targets to be reached on the way to achieving these broad objectives ("Go for the Goal," *Planning Review*, March 1997).

An objective would be to increase sacrament meeting attendance by five percent. Goals would be specific results in order to achieve the objective, such as activate four less-active families or increase the number of temple recommend holder by four by June 1. Usually the file leader and other leaders agree on the major objectives. Organizational progress often necessitates modified, new, or different objectives, so that leaders and people are not continually doing the same things the same way and achieving the same results. Goals are achieved by the individuals in the organization. Determining and achieving goals is an ongoing activity.

Goals are future expectations carried in one's mind or as written statements. We all have goals that we want to achieve concerning our desires and ambitions. Without goals we would atrophy and die.

---

**Insight: Growing, improving, and progressing
necessitates achieving goals.**

---

Goals add excitement and progress to our lives. When goals are important, few, and focused, they become a guidance system to help accomplish that which we desire to do. Accomplishing goals gives credibility to our lives.

In order for goals to be effective they should be designed according to the **smart** formula:

## SPECIFIC

## MEASURABLE

## ACHIEVABLE

## RELEVANT

## TARGETED

## ————PLANNING FOR SUCCESS————

During a stake conference assignment with a member of the Twelve, we were going over some statical information with the stake presidency. The member of the Twelve asked the stake president, "How many less-active members are there in your stake?" The stake president gave a figure, and the member of the Twelve responded, "What is your plan for activating these less-active members?" The stake president begin to talk about the less-active members in his stake. The member of the Twelve asked again "What is your plan?" The stake president looked at his counselors for a response, which did not come. It was obvious the stake president did not have a plan. He had a lot of comments and talk, but no plan.

When leaders neglect planning, they also neglect standards against which they can judge their progress and success. President Kimball used to remind leaders to "Do it with a plan."

Great achievements start with a dream, are created with a plan, and get accomplished with people.

**There are many types of leaders:**

**1. The leader who never dreams, just exists.**
**2. The leader who dreams but does not act.**
**3. The leader who dreams, believes, and acts.**
**4. The leader who dreams and helps others achieve their dreams.**

We have two choices: We can fold our arms and succumb to mediocrity and complacency, or we can think, plan, and achieve.

Some leaders succumb to organizational mediocrity and complacency, while others think and plan how to achieve their dreams. Great achievers are planners. They realize that self-discipline and planning is necessary to achieve desired results. Great achievers do not continually live in the past or justify present conditions. They plan and focus on future achievements.

Planning is a means of achieving and should not be a means of ridged control. Too great a passion for planning can stifle creativity and flexibility of performance. Planning is necessary, but there must always be adaptability because conditions will arise which necessitate flexibility, change, or new direction. Planning must always leave space for innovative leadership.

---

> **Insights: Achievers are continually moving on to better and greater achievements.**

---

Achievers are planners who cause a spirit of enthusiasm which is felt among all the people in the organization.

**Leaders who are planners:**

**1. Think and determine major objectives.**
**2. Empower those with whom they work to achieve the objectives.**
**3. Go the extra mile in thought and actions to achieve the objectives.**

Planning produces a positive, achieving climate. People are motivated to become achievers in a motivating climate where energies are directed toward their work and not misdirected toward emotional survival. When people feel valued, they also feel a spirit of freedom and are motivated to achieve planned and expected results. Planning helps build achievers.

**People are motivated to become achievers:**

**1. With a leader who gives them an opportunity to grow.**
**2. With a leader who is sensitive to their needs and potential.**
**3. With a leader who has a vision and identifies expected results.**
**4. With a leader who empowers people to succeed.**

**(1) Plan future direction, (2) determine important objectives, (3) plan for success, and you will turn on the power in your organization.**

# THE POWER OF PLANNING
## [PREPARING AN ACHIEVEMENT PLAN]

## KEY LEADERS DRAFT AN ACHIEVEMENT PLAN
1. Mental exertion: How can we improve our overall performance?
2. Determine major objectives and a plan to achieve the objectives.
3. Reach agreement why the proposed objectives are important.

## LEADERSHIP TEAM FINALIZES THE PLAN AND OBJECTIVES
1. All leaders make their suggestions and improvements concerning the objective and plans.
2. All leaders discuss and determine methods and tasks to achieve the desired objectives.
3. All leaders agree to the plan and the achievement of the objectives.

## COMMUNICATE THE PLAN AND OBJECTIVES
1. Where we are now and where do we want to be in the future?
2. How can we get to where we want to be?
3. Why are achieving the plan and objectives important?

## IMPLEMENT THE PLAN
1. Communicate the desired outcome to all participating people.
2. Outline in detail how progress and improvement will be tracked and monitored.
3. Identify who is accountable to achieve the objectives and the methods of reporting on results.

# THE POWER OF
# EFFECTIVE OPERATIONS

"Effective management is the art of
multiplying yourself through others."
(*The Teachings of Ezra Taft Benson,* p. 68).

My wife, Donna, and I arrived early one evening to attend a symphony concert. While sitting in the audience, we watched and listened to the musicians prepare themselves and their instruments for the concert. Each participant in the orchestra was checking his or her instrument—violin, tuba, flute, cornet, and so on.

Frankly, the sounds were not pleasant. What we heard was a mass of musical confusion—all the instruments were out of harmony with one another as each one played a different part of the music to be presented during the concert. I remember thinking while I listened that some organizations are like that orchestra, each organizational unit doing its own thing, lacking unity, direction, and purpose.

However, when the conductor entered and stood before the orchestra, each person stopped doing his own thing and focused his attention on the conductor. He raised his baton and the participants began to play, united in amazing harmony, each one playing a separate piece but in concert with the whole group.

The music they played was beautiful. The orchestra was united in working together to accomplish a single purpose. The conductor was aware of each musician as his eyes scanned the entire group. He not only observed the total group but was aware of each person in the group and the part each played.

Each member of the group was intent on fulfilling the conductor's expectations. His purpose was to present a perfect concert, one that would please each member of the orchestra and the listening audience.

He knew the strengths and the performance ability of each musician. He also knew that together they could produce an outstanding concert. They wanted to achieve the expectations of the conductor.

Peter Drucker said:

> "[A] manager's first task is to make effective the strengths of people, and this he can do only if he starts out with the assumption that people—and especially managers—want to achieve" (*Management, Tasks, Responsibilities, and Practices,* p. 441).

A leader of an organization can do and be as successful as the conductor of the orchestra if he is effective in:

# 1. MONITORING PEOPLE PERFORMANCE
# 2. GUIDING OPERATIONAL UNITS
# 3. FOLLOWING UP ON EXPECTED RESULTS

## ——MONITORING PEOPLE PERFORMANCE——

An organization can be likened to the physical body. The body is made up of functional parts all tied together as a working unit. The mind and the heart are the two key or primary areas that have the greatest effect on the functioning of the body. The central nervous system carries information throughout the body. When all the parts of the body are working harmoniously, you have a healthy active person.

When something goes wrong with the physical body, the person may be taken to the hospital. As the doctor and nurses check on their patients regularly, they begin by checking the medical chart hanging on the end of the bed. After studying the chart, the medical professional checks the patient's vital signs while they discuss the patient's perceptions of what is happening with his or her body. When the physical problems are identified and resolved, the patient leaves the hospital a revitalized person.

An organization is a group of units tied together as a working group, similar to the structure of an orchestra and the human body. At times the organization needs to be examined and the operating parts of the organization checked to see how they are doing. The leader checks organizational statistics, trends, certain vital signs, and attitudes to determine if all units are working unitedly and are on the planned course to achieve determined objectives.

Although it is important to check regularly statistical information, do not get hung up on judging organizational health by numbers alone. Statistical data are just symbols that represent the collective behavior of a group of people. Use such information to look for the trends—how is the organization moving? What trends are moving upward? What activities have come to rest on a plateau or are moving downward relative to expected outcomes? Determine what is happening, why it is happening, what needs to be improved, and then take the appropriate action to make the needed improvements. Check the organizational vital signs by talking to people: ask questions, observe attitudes, notice body language, listen to conversations, and note people dispositions.

---

**Insight: Statistical data symbolize the collective behavior of the people.**

---

Operating units function as integral parts of the total organization. The pro-active leader will always take the time to carefully analyze each operating unit and determine how it is doing in accomplishing the purpose of the unit and the vision and purpose of the organization. Recognize that every unit in an organization will produce results. However, the results may or may not be in harmony with the file leader's desired outcome. The point is, people will produce results, either their own or those of their file leader. An effective leader will provide clear, attainable objectives for his organization to strive for in keeping with the overall purpose of the organization.

One way leader might monitor his organization's activities is to check on the expected outcomes of each unit. Determine whether they are just doing activities or are achieving important results. In so doing, you will develop "improvement awareness" and see that right things are being accomplished. Keep in mind, if you want improved outcomes, you must improve the way current outcomes are being achieved. Determining and improving new and different outcomes necessitates prayer and receiving divine inspiration, organizational awareness, and problem solving skills.

Solving problems is a product of progress. Problems come in many different ways, but there are mainly two kinds of problems:

**Maintenance problems**, which are usually obvious, including things that need to be done now in order to maintain effective operations. Maintenance problems would include rounding up additional chairs because more people came to a fireside than were anticipated, talking to an upset member or arranging a ride for a stranded quorum member. Solving maintenance problems is an ongoing daily activity of an active leader.

**Maintenance problems are identified by awareness:**

**1. Seeing problem conditions.**
**2. Hearing problem concerns.**
**3. Listening to problem complaints.**

Solving maintenance problems happens when a leader moves out from behind his desk and walks and talks with people—sensing, feeling and learning what is going on with the people, and becoming mindful of attitudes, feelings, and dispositions of people in the organization.

**Problem Solving**, determining how to achieve improved and accomplish new outcomes. There may be a need for new direction and new objectives. Problem-solving is much more than making things right when they go wrong. Solving problems necessitates inspiration in overcoming existing non-productive conditions and creating new conditions in order to achieve new and important results.

**Problem Solving is identified by asking questions:**

**1. What new and specific outcome do we want to achieve?**
**2. What obstacles are standing in our way?**
**3. What action must we take now?**

Problem solving happens when organizational values encourage innovative thinking, motivated achievers, and attitudes of venture. Such values encourage creative thinking, taking cautious risks for improvement and achievement. This leads to people showing initiative to achieve new objectives, as well as spending time and energy praying and thinking of how to achieve new and different outcomes in order to accomplish the mission of the church. As people experience success, they feel rewarded for achieving organization results and strive to evaluate what must next be accomplished—and thus begins the recurring positive cycle of solving problems.

---

**Insight: you cannot keep doing the same things the same way and expect changed conditions and improved results.**

---

# ———GUIDING OPERATIONAL UNITS———

While a stake president was driving me to the airport, he asked me a very good question, "How can I get out from under all the people problems? I find myself involved in doing for people that which they can do for themselves." I suggested to him that he should not get totally away from working with people, for that was his stewardship. But I realized that people will too often call on a stake president or a bishop before they first try to solve their own problems.

I told him about a bishop who, when people came to him for his counsel, didn't just sit and counsel with them; rather, after he listened to their problems he gave them counsel that always included a specific assignment that would take time and effort and would help them with their problem. For example, to a couple having problems getting along, he might say, "Before we meet again, will you read 3 Nephi and ponder what the Lord says about contention?" To a couple learning to deal with challenging children, he might ask, "Will you as parents start holding weekly parent planning meetings so that you can be united in your relationships with your children?" To a struggling returned missionary, he might request, "During the next month will you go to the temple once each week, and in the temple count your many blessings and ponder them one by one?" This bishop did two important things: (1) he gave those whom he counseled important and worthwhile assignments, and (2) he always asked "Will you..." questions that required a commitment to some measurable result. In doing so, he created an environment in which the people could solve their own problems.

When the individual or couple called for another interview, he or his executive secretary would always ask, "Have you completed the assignment you were given during the last interview?" If they hadn't, he would ask them, in a kind manner, to complete the assignment and then call again for an appointment.

**The bishop improved his counseling and saved his time in three ways:**

1. **He gave them an assignment that was important and took time and effort to do.**
2. **The assignments he gave them would help them overcome their problem.**
3 **He reduced the frequency of his counseling interviews.**

The stake president thanked me and said he felt that could help him and his bishops. Then he asked: "I can see how your counsel will help me not to do for people what they can do for themselves. I also find it frustrating when people seem to want me to do their thinking for them to solve their problems. Do you have any suggestions that can help me with this problem?" I mentioned to him some other methods I had learned from other stake presidents and bishops. I suggested that he:

**Practice asking three important questions:**

**1. What am I doing that I can delegate to others?**
**2. When asked for advice, ask: "What do you think?"**
**3. When a person presents problems always ask, "What is your recommendation for solving this problem?"**

**Asking these reflective questions causes four things to happen:**

**1. People assume greater responsibility.**
**2. People learn to think before they ask questions.**
**3. The leader is required to handle fewer problems.**
**4. People become empowered to solve their own problems.**

File leaders need to plan structured times to meet with their subordinate or unit leaders. Structured meetings give subordinate or unit leaders an opportunity to report their progress and file leaders the opportunity to make course corrections as needed. Listen with interest and give proper recognition, gratitude, and appreciation.

See yourself as a loving, caring parent with the desire to see each member of the organizational family learn his or her responsibilities, grow, and produce right results. Allow people to function with a minimum of interference, but be available to help when needed.

President Harold B. Lee frequently quoted Doctrine and Covenants 107:99, "Wherefore, now let every man learn his duty, and to act in the office in which he is appointed, in all diligence." His follow-up comments usually emphasized the word *let* in this scripture. He indicated that we must *let* people learn their duty, not do for them that which they can do for themselves.

It has been my experience that if we do not take time to train people to learn their duty, and then let them do it, we often have to use our time to solve their problems. We actually save time by knowing what each individual unit leader is expected to achieve, and then ensuring that he or she is properly trained to fulfil their responsibilities and achieve your expectations as their leader.

**If you want to get the best results from people:**

**1. Communicate *what* you expect.**
**2. Communicate *when* you expect it.**
**3. Communicate *who* you expect to achieve the results.**

---

**Insight: People will rise to the expectation of their leader.**

---

**Problem-Solving Method**

Maintaining effective operations requires effective problem solving. To be effective in solving problems, you must be sure to get all the facts. A wise file leader once said that if you don't get all the facts, the facts will get you. Get the facts by talking to people, studying the situation from different angles, learn the history of the problem, obtain more than one person's point of view.

**To solve problems consider the following questions:**

**1. Is it best to let this problem work itself out without my inter-ference?**
**2. Is the trend of the problem growing or declining?**
**3. Is the problem best handled by action or no action?**

If the decision is to take action, consider the following steps:

1. The problem is:

_____

_____

_____

2. The affects of the problem are:

_____

_____

_____

3. Which is causing the following:

_____

_____

_____

4. A successful solution to the problem is:

_____

_____

_____

---

> **Insight: The crucial act for solving problems
> is to get all the facts.**

---

# ——FOLLOW UP ON EXPECTED RESULTS——

Some of the best follow-up artists are mothers. They delegate work for their children to do and then follow up to see that the work is done.

**I see at least four reasons for a mother's effectiveness:**

1.  **She wants her child to learn how to do things right.**
2.  **She wants her child to learn to accept responsibility and to be accountable.**
3.  **She wants to save herself time by having her child help do the work.**
4.  **She feels a responsibility to teach and train her child.**

We can become more effective leaders if we will follow the example of most mothers in training their children. Unfortunately, as I expressed earlier, many Church leaders spend more time dealing with problems than achieving results. The more progressive leader solves problems by thinking in terms of achieving results. He realizes that most problems occur because people have not accomplished the right results.

Leaders who delegate work should also determine the end result to be achieved. It is easy to delegate but not so easy to follow up. However, following up can be as easy as asking a person, "How are you doing?" When convenient, allow the person to whom you are delegating to set his or her own completion dates: "When *will you* complete this assignment?" When you let assigned individuals set the time for completing the assignment, he will be more inclined to follow through and complete the assignment according to his established time line.

---

**Insight: Delegation without follow-up is abdication.**

---

In order to ensure progress, there is need for freedom to experiment, to try new methods and ideas; inevitably these trials may result in some mistakes. Progress stops when everyone in an organization is afraid to try something new or do something different for fear of making a mistake and being chastised by their file leader.

Encourage people to try new, reasonable approaches, *new* being synonymous with growth. You can help people "feel" they have the freedom to try new things without fear of reprimand when you establish guide lines and show a willingness to listen to their ideas. Some mistakes are a cheap price to pay for growth and progress of an individual or an organization. When encouraging people:

**Keep in mind:**

**1. Orders and commands stir resentment.**
**2. Explaining stirs progress:**
**3. Listening builds confidence**
**4. Appreciation builds success**

The most important responsibility to be accomplished is to delegate the specific, measurable results to be achieved. The second most important responsibility is to follow up and make sure delegated results are completed. Remember, what you expect, you have to inspect.

Establishing methods of follow-up is imperative if you want to keep an organization alive and moving. There are often many important tasks that are delegated and then forgotten because of lack of follow up. I listened to a Stake president in a training meeting teach the principle of follow up when he referred to Abraham and the creation of the earth. He said the creation of the earth was not left to chance there was continual follow up to see things were done right. Then he quoted from Abraham 4: 18, "And the Gods watched those things which they had ordered until they obeyed."

Effective follow up helps a leader to see more clearly what is happening in the organization and know the effectiveness of the people. Follow up is essential for getting right things done, yet follow-up is one of the most neglected principles of leadership. It is much easier to delegate than to follow up. The only sure way to know if a task is completed is to establish procedures for follow up.

---
**Insight: People may neglect what you expect,
but they will do what you inspect.**

---

The more bonded the relationship with individuals and groups, the more likely they will achieve your expectations. Bonding happens when you are positive and build positive relationships, when you communicate with understanding, when your delegated assignments are clear with specific results to be achieved and suggestions for follow up.

**You will get the expected results when you:**

**1. Interview with purpose and intent.**
**2. Teach pertinent principles.**
**3. Ask "will you?" questions when you make assignments.**
**4. Follow up with thanks and appreciation.**

To effectively achieve your desired outcome, you need effective methods of follow up. The following are some suggestions:

1. **The agenda.** Note delegated action items, to whom, follow up in the next meeting.
2. **Calendaring.** Items calendared with a starting date and ending date are usually completed.
3. **Secretaries and Clerks.** Secretaries or clerks are assigned to track all follow-up items.
4. **Reporting.** Establish reporting dates and a time to evaluate their progress.
5. **Interviews.** Calendar date and times for interim progress reports.
6. **Meetings.** An important time to follow up with a progress report.
7. **Minutes.** The agenda items become the outline for the minutes of the meeting.
8. **Follow-up chart**: _____

| Assignment | Person Assigned | Date Assigned | Due Date | Date Completed | Comments |
|---|---|---|---|---|---|
|  |  |  |  |  |  |

The less observant you are to what is happening in each unit in the organization, the more you will think and feel that everything is okay. The observant leader sees and feels the pulse of each unit in the organization. He invests himself in what is happening in order to be more aware of what is happening. He shows interest, gives encouragement, and expresses appreciation while following up on expected results.

**Improve how you (1) monitor people performance, (2) guide operational units, and (3) establish follow-up procedures. You will achieve the expected results and turn on the power in your organization.**

# POWER OF EFFECTIVE OPERATIONS

|  | Agree | Disagree |
|---|---|---|
| 1. Everyone in the organization shows commitment to the purpose and vision of the organization. | _____ | _____ |
| 2. Each unit shows consistency in direction. | _____ | _____ |
| 3. The competence of the organization and its units are recognizable by other people's comments. | _____ | _____ |
| 4. People in the organization and unit know what is expected of them and are achieving the expectations. | _____ | _____ |
| 5. Individuals are encouraged to see and solve problems. | _____ | _____ |
| 6. Leaders "walk and talk" the purpose and vision of the organization. | _____ | _____ |
| 7. Leaders show gratitude and appreciation. | _____ | _____ |

# THE POWER OF MOTIVATION

"Life is from within outward,
and never from without inward,
You are the center of power in your own life"
(Ernest Holmes, *Creative Mind and Success*, p. 37).

Donna and I raised four boys and one girl. We wanted our children to share in the responsibilities of our home. To motivate them to share in the work responsibilities, we prepared a weekly work sheet that outlined the different jobs we wanted the children to do. We soon found out that the work sheet worked only for a while. Telling them did not always get things done. Yelling did get things done, when accompanied by close supervision, but it only worked for a very short period of time and always caused a negative relationship with little cooperation and very little learning.

After years of trial, error, and study, we learned some things about motivation. We learned that human behavior is goal directed. We realized there is a cause for the existing behavior. If a child did not want to clean his room, it was because the child was goal directed to do something that to him was more important than a clean room. When we determined the goal he had in his mind, we could use that goal to motivate or negotiate and get things done.

Our responsibility was to first determine the goal that caused each child's behavior. Then we could adjust our behavior so that we could better influence their behavior to motivate them to get things done. We also learned that praise and recognition for work well done made it easer to get the same work done at another time. We learned that each of our children had different kinds of motivations, and we had to understand and recognize each of their talents and abilities. Once we recognized their individuality, we were in a better situation to create appropriate motivation and give recognition to get things done.

---

**Insight: You receive more of the behavior that you reward.**

---

Learning about motivation in our family is similar to a leader's learning about motivating people in an organization. The challenges are similar—both require taking time to know people and to recognize their individual motivations and goals. Knowing people is necessary for leaders to motivate people. To motivate others the leader must first be self-motivated. People are more inclined to follow a self-motivated leader.

**Three important areas of motivation are:**

# 1. SELF-MOTIVATION
# 2. PEOPLE MOTIVATION
# 3. ORGANIZATIONAL MOTIVATION

## ———SELF-MOTIVATION———

Self-motivation in simple terms is victory over self. It is the ability to manage yourself against self-opposition and the opposition of other people. When it comes to serving the Lord, there is a lot of opposition. We need help, spiritual power, revelation, and divine guidance to motivate us to do what we know we should do. While serving as a temple president I observed a stake president who attended the temple regularly. One evening while visiting with him I commented on how regularly he attended the temple. He said, "I don't think I could effectively preside over our stake if I did not calendar regularly attendance at the temple." He continued, "I do not attend the temple just when it is convenient; I attend regularly because I have found that the influence of the Spirit in the temple, the reminder of my covenants, and the service rendered to those on the other side of the veil has a positive influence upon my spirit. Because of attending the temple regularly I feel that I receive a greater power of discernment, insights, specific revelation, and increased wisdom in my calling as the stake president."

In my own leadership experience and visiting with stake presidents, I have learned that to turn on the spiritual motivating power in our life and calling, it is important to do the following:

**1. Attend the temple regularly.**
**2. Read the scriptures regularly.**
**3. Study the words of the prophets regularly.**
**4. On fast day, fast with a purpose regularly.**

If you are too busy to do these four things, then you are too busy.

---

| **Insight: Successful people do what failures don't want to do.** |
| --- |

---

## FOUR CHARACTERISTICS OF A MOTIVATED PERSON

My first appointment for the morning was with a young man who worked in our office. We visited for a few minutes, then I asked, "How can I help you?" He said, "I just can't seem to get myself motivated. I have great desire; but when it comes to actual performance I do not do as I feel I should do." I congratulated him on his desire to improve. Knowing him to be a devoted worker, I reminded him that he was focusing too much on his weaknesses, whereas he should be focusing more on his strengths. He said, "Okay, but how can I better motivate myself?" I then suggested that he adopt the following four characteristics of a self-motivated person:

## 1. Create a daily list of "to do" items, prioritize them, then do the important items first.

Charles Schwab, who was president of Bethlehem Steel, told of an efficiency expert, Ive Lee, who wanted to sell Schwab on how to become more efficient. Schwab was not interested, but he was willing to try one idea for one month that Lee suggested would make him more efficient. If the idea was of value, he would send Ive Lee a check for what he felt the idea was worth. Schwab tried the idea for one month, after which he was so impressed with what the idea had helped him accomplish that he sent Lee a check for $25,000.

Ive Lee asked Schwab to daily list the items that he had to do each day and prioritize them, with the most important item at the top of the list. Then he was to focus his attention on completing the most important item first and not concern himself about the less-important items until the number one item was finished.

I explained to my young friend that Ive Lee's suggestion was the forerunner to the planning book many executives carry around with them. I indicated to him that I used 3"x5" cards to write down information, a habit I developed before planning books were available in such commercial abundance. Whenever something of importance pops into my mind—morning, day, or evening—I write it on my 3"x5" card. Each morning I determined what I wanted to accomplish that day. I then underlined the most important items. I informed him that consistency in prioritizing my "to do" list helped me to better manage my time, get important things done, and feel good about myself.

## 2. Return and Report. No Excuses.

A number of years ago I learned a great lesson. I had the good fortune to serve for a number of years as the secretary to the Quorum of the Twelve Apostles. One day towards the beginning of my service, I was in the office of one of the Twelve. We were discussing a number of items, and I was listening with real intent when he stopped the conversation and asked, "Rulon, when you come to my office, do you

want me to furnish you with a pad and pencil, or will you bring your own?" I was embarrassed but learned a very important lesson—never be without something to take notes on.

I have since always carried in my shirt pocket two or three 3"x5" cards. Whenever I was in a conversation with someone—whether in an office or the hallway—I was always ready to write down any items that were important for me to follow up on. I also found that 3"x5" cards in my shirt pocket were valuable to help me remember any ideas, insights, or inspiration that I might receive throughout the day.

I suggested to the young man, "When you are given something to do, the person delegating the assignment to you always likes to see you make a note of the item to be done. He will also be interested in knowing the progress and the outcome. A note, a memo, or phone call as soon as possible after completing the assignment is always appreciated. The practice of writing things down, doing them, and reporting back as soon as possible will bring you the compliment, 'He is quick and accurate.'"

## 3. Quick and Accurate

A principle of effectiveness is that when you receive an assignment, do it. Soon! Don't procrastinate. If it can be done now, then do it now. If not now, put it on a list of priority items.

Develop the practice and create the habit of never being asked twice to do something. Keep the person who delegated the item to you informed on how you are progressing. He then knows you have not forgotten and are progressing to its completion. Delegated items should be completed as quickly and accurately as possible. Then you can get on with your own work, which is always less important than that work delegated to you from your file leader.

## 4. The Still, Small Voice

I explained to the young man that the greatest motivation principle is to listen to the still, small voice and do as it prompts. Obedience to the still, small voice is the most important principle of self-motivation. If you act on inspiration received, you will continue to receive more and greater inspiration. But if you do not act on that inspiration, the still, small voice will become dimmer and dimmer in your life. The voice of the Holy Spirit will increasingly guide and direct your life and activities when you obey the inspiration that you have already received.

I indicated to the young man that if he would consistently do these four things for one month, he would create a good habit of self-motivation and overcome the habit of procrastination. His desire and willingness to improve his self-motivation would outweigh the habit of procrastination. I concluded our conversation by telling him that in my opinion, the only motivation is self-motivation. You can be inspired by the still, small voice and by other people, but they cannot make you do what you have to do or should do. Self-motivation starts and ends with you.

> **Insight: Leaders are impressed by what you do,**
> **not what you neglect to do.**

## YOUR PERSONAL ACHIEVEMENT PLAN

We all carry in our mind mental images of what we would like to do and become. However, most people who fantasize about becoming an achieving person lack the motivation to do so. They are complacent with what they are now doing. Their mental fantasizing is mental pseudo-activity without effort.

Complacency is the enemy of achievement. As long as you are satisfied with things as they now are—and as you now are—you will not have the motivation to do what you want to do or become what you want to become. The road to personal achievement and improvement is to learn from your past experiences and the experiences of others and strive to do better and become better. Prepare a list of three to five things you want to improve on or achieve. Avoid generalities like making more money or becoming more successful. Be specific, and prioritize your list with the most important objective first. **Then:**

**1. Excite your imagination with your desire for greater achievement.**
**2. Make a plan for achieving what you want to achieve and become.**
**3. Practice self-leadership. Do what is necessary. In the doing comes the power.**

The price for achievement is paid for in advance in thought, effort, time, and discipline.

There is no credit card approach to personal achievement—you have to pay the price first. The test of achievement is when you are continually making some physical effort toward what you want to achieve.

---

**Insight: Think about what you will do,
rather than what you won't do.**

---

## ———PEOPLE MOTIVATION———

I was sitting on the stand next to a stake president right before stake conference began; as we looked over the large audience, he asked: "How do you motivate groups of people?" I replied that many successful leaders use the IEFF method. When he asked what that was, I suggested that after the meeting we could discuss it. After that session of the conference was over, we retired to the president's office, where I wrote vertically down the white board the letters IEFF:

## IDENTIFY
## EXPECT
## FOCUS
## FOLLOW THROUGH

We discussed each of the above phases and how they motivate people to act:

**Identify** When people know and understand what the most important things are to achieve, they are more motivated to achieve those things.

**Expect** When a leader outlines what is expected—that is, the end results to accomplish—people are more motivated to achieve the desired results of the leader.

**Focus** When people are focused on achieving expected results, they pay attention to doing the right things.

**Follow through** When a leader follows through on what he expects, he increases the faith in people to support his leadership.

---

**Insight: Groups are motivated by success.**

---

When our children were young, working on the Church welfare farm was always a part of our summer activity. I learned a great lesson from the approach of two different bishops as they motivated the members of their respective wards to work on the welfare farm. When it came time to pick the fruit on the welfare farm, one bishop reminded the ward members that they were to be at the farm on a specific day and time. He went on to somewhat criticize the members for not being more valiant in serving on the welfare farm and firmly suggested that they needed to do better. Our boys listened and groaned at the thought of getting up early in the morning to pick fruit.

The next bishop had a different approach. The week before it was time to pick fruit on the Church farm, he and his counselors spoke in the sacrament meeting on the doctrine of welfare. They explained why the Church welfare program was established, the purpose of the welfare program, and how the welfare products that were picked on our farm were used. I overheard one of our boys say to the other, "I didn't know that." The bishop was the last speaker, and he asked each family on Monday night during their family home evening to further discuss the doctrine of welfare.

In our family home evening we were able to answer questions from our children and further teach them the related doctrines, as the bishop had suggested. What was of great interest to me was that our children did not moan and grown; instead they got up early, and as a family we went to the welfare farm to pick fruit. While picking fruit one of our boys was singing. A friend ask me why he seemed happy and was singing. I told him he was happy and singing because he understood the doctrine of welfare. The lesson I learned is that *teaching the doctrine motivates.*

---

**Insight: Lack of motivation is often lack of information.**

---

While visiting with a stake president I asked him what his profession was? He told me he was in the training business. When I pursued a bit further, he shared with me the type of training he did. I asked him to teach me what he felt was an effective training principle. He asked me if I had heard of the 100 monkey theory. After I responded that I had not, he explained to me the 100 monkey theory.

A group of social scientists wanted to change the behavior of 100 monkeys, so they selected 10 bright monkeys. They effectively trained the 10 bright monkeys in what was expected of them, that is, a new behavior. Then the scientists used the 10 bright monkeys to influence and change the behavior of the other 90 monkeys. He said that the 100 monkey theory is a basic principle of effective training and motivation. The leader selects a few willing and motivated people and trains them well in what the leader expects; then he assigns them to go out and train others. He said that in his stake he focused on effectively training the leaders and expected them to train others. The 100 monkey theory is the power of proper example.

I asked what he would do if the training did not meet expectations. "In that case," he said, "we continue to retrain our leaders until they make a difference."

---

**Insight: When you assign me to do something,
without training me you frustrate me.**

---

Motivation take place in the mind and heart of people when a leader's example shows consistency of action, fairness in decisions, and dedication to unselfish objectives. People are motivated to achieve planned objectives when they have respect for their leader, who shows by his actions that he is an inspired leader. Respect is earned by being a proper example.

In order to motivate others to help you reach your objectives, they must believe in the importance of the objective. If they do not believe what you want to accomplish is reasonable and attainable, they will lack the motivation to help you achieve your objective. It is important that you know and communicate:

**1. What you want to achieve.**
**2. Who can best help you to achieve it.**
**3. Ask, "Will you do it?"**

The following questions can lead to a positive discussion in helping to motivate and empower people to improve their performance and help you to achieve your important objectives.

**1. What in your calling is your highest priority?**
**2. Do you feel you are progressing in your responsibilities?**
**3. How can you do better?**
**4. What areas are you striving to improve?**
**5. What will you do better next month?**
**6. How can I help you?**

# ———ORGANIZATIONAL MOTIVATION———

Motivation depends on creating clear objectives that people can see, feel, and achieve. An objective is a motive to act. The motive to act becomes stronger when the objective harmonizes with individual goals and the mission of the organization. In the Church, members are motivated when their personal goals help achieve the mission of the

Church, and when they feel trust and confidence in their leader. Some key principles for building trust, confidence, and motivating people are:

**Your smile.** A smile stimulates within you and within others a pleasant feeling, a pleasant attitude. No matter how bad you feel, when you smile you feel better. And when you feel better, people around you feel better.

## SMILE AND THE WORLD SMILES WITH YOU; FROWN AND YOU FROWN ALONE.

Inner happiness is manifest in your smile. It takes more facial muscles to frown than it does to smile, and most people are overworked! A friendly smile radiates appreciation and a calmness of mind and action. A smile and a friendly handshake or pat on the back motivates people and lets them know that you like and appreciate them. Your smile is a result of choice. Remember to smile.

---

**Insight: You are not fully dressed until you are wearing your smile.**

---

When you smile, it enhances your charm with people. Your smiling countenance is your shop window to your inner world. If you don't feel like a smile, fake it and make a smile. Smiling has great motivating power. Your smile is the advertisement of your personality.

When you smile at people, aren't you impressed to see their answering smiles? When you smile at a person, you make that person happy. We all love the person that smiles and makes us smile and feel happy. If you see someone without a smile, give them one of yours.

**Positive information.** Positive information is an essential part of good motivation. Good communication means keeping individuals informed on what is happening, what they need to know, how they are doing. Good communication unlocks the potential in other people's lives.

When people do not have enough information to make an effective judgment, they often fear to make a decision or are not sure how to act, so they tend to assume the worst and lack motivation. People assuming the worst is the first step in creating a negative environment. Positive and reassuring communication accompanied with understanding is a powerful motivator.

---

**Insight: Understanding and being understood motivates.**

---

**Shared Information** Understanding is what happens when individuals have the opportunity to share information with each other. People sharing information with each other causes a sense of connection. Effective leaders create opportunities for sharing information that leads to greater understanding. The more people understands why a task is needed and expected, the greater will be their motivation to accomplish the delegated tasks. Making time to share information is a vital part of successful group motivation. Shared information brings understanding and the motivation to do what is expected.

**Goals.** Many organizations find reward motivation an effective way to motivate a group of people. Reward motivations can be depicted by a donkey pulling a cart with a carrot dangling from a stick in front of the donkey. Reward motivation is external motivation and is often effective. The challenge however is determining and maintaining new, different, and greater rewards to keep people motivated. A higher level of motivation is internal motivation. Internal motivation is based on personal worthiness, desire, positive attitude, and internal determination. A group performs best when they want to, not because of reprimand or reward.

Internal motivation is achieved and maintained when people know who they are and what they can become. It is built on internal and eternal beliefs in achieving goals that will bring about self-improvement, growth, and personal recognition to the individual and the organization. Without goals individuals tend to feel that activity alone is accomplishment. Goals become important when they set direction for the organization and are a means of achieving individual dreams, desires, and future accomplishments. Emerson said it best: "No one ever accomplished anything of consequence without a goal." Goals are accomplished when a leader realizes that effectively teaching the doctrine with understanding motivates individuals to achieve goals.

**Love people.** The greatest of all motivation is love. We are taught to love God and to love people. To love people and the work you have been called to do is to love life. Love is a power that is unsurpassed in motivating people. To love a person is to want to see that person grow, be happy, and succeed. To trust people with responsibility and recognize them for their achievements is an indication of motivating love.

To love people is to motivate people. Love is energy—it creates positive feelings and builds the spirit of harmony among people in an organization. Love encourages an effectual interest in the well-being of people. Positive support and encouragement and showing love and appreciation, along with recognition, praise, and thanks, is absolutely necessary to cause people to feel valued and motivated to do what is necessary. Continually look for the positives in what people do.

Leaders do not have a lot of time with the people they serve; therefore the time spent with them must be quality time. If your instructions are to take root in the mind and heart of the people you must instruct with kindness and sensitivity which will cause people to respond to your instructions and be motivated to do what you desire them to do. To make it happen people must feel it needs to happen and be recognized and appreciated for making it happen.

---

**Insight: Motivated people make a difference.**

---

**You will turn on the power in your organization when you are (1) self-motivated, (2) create people motivation, and (3) promote organizational motivation.**

# THE POWER OF MOTIVATION

## <u>Motivation happens when people feel needed, cared about, and challenged.</u>

**People are motivated in a positive climate that encourages self-effort.**
1. Open communication is evident throughout the organization.
2. People feel you are interested in their growth and development.
3. People feel at ease because of a positive and friendly working environment.
4. People feel valued and respected for themselves and the work they accomplish.

**What you are as a leader is more motivating than what you do as a leader.**
1. People are treated with courtesy.
2. People feel you are encouraging and helpful in their work.
3. People feel that you are approachable.
4. People feel you want them to succeed.

**You motivate people to be effective achievers when:**
1. People know what is expected of them.
2. People have goals to achieve.
3. People are given specific responsibilities and held accountable.
4. People are being challenged.

# THE POWER OF SYSTEMS

"Whatever course you decide upon,
there is always someone to tell you that you are wrong.
There are always difficulties arising which tempt you
to believe that your critics are right.
To map out a course of action and
follow it to an end requires courage."

Ralph Waldo Emerson

You may have heard the story of the poor farmer who set out to plow a field one spring morning. It was an important job that needed to be done that day. He started out early to oil his tractor and found he needed more oil, so he went to the barn to get it. On the way to the barn, he noticed that the pigs had not been fed. Therefore, he went to the corn crib, where he saw some sacks lying on the floor. Seeing the sacks reminded him that the potatoes were sprouting, so he started for the potato pit. As he passed the wood pile, he remembered his wife wanted some wood for the house. While he was picking up some wood, he spotted a chicken that was ailing, so he dropped the wood and went to its aid. When evening arrived, the tractor was still in the barn and the field was still unplowed. The poor farmer had worked hard all day but had not accomplished the most important job.

Some leaders are much like the poor farmer. They work hard all day but often do not get the most important things done. Part of the reason is that they are not motivated to achieve an objective or, like the farmer, are distracted by less important things. Organizing systems within an organization is a way to more effectively arrange, prioritize, and manage to get important things done first.

A system is a set of procedures linked together in order to do or accomplish something. A system brings about order by tying together fragmented parts, or different functions, into a working relationship to accomplish a purpose or objective.

In this chapter, I will attempt to explain system thinking and organizing. I know from personal experience that creating systems to get things done helps for an effective, smooth running organization.

Three ingredients that have helped me to understand and organize a system are:

# 1. ANALYZE
# 2. ORGANIZE
# 3. SYSTEMATIZE

## ———ANALYZE———

The poor farmer in the story had an important job to do. He saw the many things that needed to be done. He was using his eyes but not his mind. Most likely his work methods were the same every day. He was neither effective nor efficient. If he had known how to analyze, organize, and systematize his work, he would have been a more efficient and effective farmer.

He needed to stop long enough to think and analyze what he was doing and what he had to do. He could then have determined what should be done that day and could organize and prioritize his work.

A skilled leader is also a skilled analyst. Such a leader not only sees what needs to be done but thinks and analyzes the best way to do it, focusing on what is most important first. Analyzing helps us see how to best organize and prioritize what needs to be done.

---

**Insight: Analyzing is a prerequisite to organizing and prioritizing.**

---

To analyze is to break something down into separate parts in order to study it. The farmer, in seeing all the work that he had to do, could have analyzed and broken his workload into parts and then organized and prioritized the parts into a system of operation. For example, he could have used the following system for prioritizing his work.

Using the letters *A* through *E,* we can create a system of categories to prioritize the work to be done, identifying that which is most important *(A)* to that which is least important *(E):*

**A - Absolutely (Must do, urgent and important.)**
**B - Better do (Do as soon as possible.)**
**C - Could do (Worth my time and effort to do.)**
**D - Delegate (Give to someone else to do.)**
**E - Eliminate (Abolish.)**

This system could have helped the farmer work more efficiently and effectively and with less frustration and stress. It establishes order for the work to be accomplished. It also establishes a motivational hierarchy for getting first things done first. If the farmer had analyzed his work, he would have seen all he had to do, and he could have better organized and systematized his work.

One of the key functions of analyzing is to define "current reality," seeing things as they really are now. The farmer did not see the current reality of the work he had to do. Understanding current reality is your springboard to new and organized effort. I have found analyzing and defining current reality to be a great motivating power in influencing right decisions, creating new attitudes, and getting the work done.

Many leaders just see the present work to be done. They do not analyze how to do it and simplify their work. Therefore, they mostly react to current events rather than being proactive to future opportunities. Current reality often presents a new cause for action.

---

**Insight: Determining current reality helps you plan future action.**

---

**To analyze is to:**

1. See the problem.
2. Determine the cause.
3. Think of possible solutions.
4. Take appropriate action.

## ————ORGANIZE————

The function of organizing is not always visible. It takes place first in the mind of the leader, behind the scenes as ongoing activity. The results of today are usually the results of organized thinking done in the past. Organization work today brings about the results of improved work tomorrow.

**The kind of behind the scenes thinking that needs to be done is:**

1. Determine current reality.
2. Establish new objectives.
3. Focus on how to achieve the new objectives.

The person whose desire is to control, gain recognition, or be the center of attention does not find time for the seclusion it takes to think, organize, and prioritize.

**To organize is to:**

1. Think.
2. Design.
3. Plan.
4. Present.

This kind of lonely work is essential for the growth and progress of an organization and its people. The leader who can think, organize, and prioritize must be able to recognize confusion and unproductive effort, gather information, make decisions, and determine action in order to achieve right results.

---

**Insight: Organizing your work is organizing your mind.**

---

## ————SYSTEMATIZE————

Often a system of work becomes routine, therefore saving thought and effort. A leader first starts by identifying a need then organizing a system to accommodate, solve, or accomplish the need. Often, right things are not accomplished because there are many different things to be done, which frustrates progress. The casual or non-thinking leader is caught up in organizational fragmentation. He encounters many different things to do, like the farmer. Each thing demands attention in different directions, causing confusion, frustration, and stress.

When we organize, prioritize, systematize, and calendar what needs to be done, we work more efficiently and effectively. Seeing the parts is one thing. Seeing how to organize the parts into a working system is the right thing. The farmer saw many things to do, but he was unable to formulate all the things to do into a system for getting done what needed to be done first.

The human body provides us with an analogy of systems and how they work. The body is made up of different systems, such as the immune system, vascular system, central nervous system, and lymphatic system. The body could never survive if these systems were not working harmoniously as both separate and integrated systems within the human body.

---

**Insight: Well-planned systems have the ability to maintain themselves.**

---

The effective leader sees the overall organization and creates and manages systems within the organization. Such a leader also sees where parts of the organization could be incorporated into other parts within a system for greater efficiency and effectiveness and to achieve desired outcomes. For example, a leader may see that some people are not working effectively or are at cross purposes with each other. The leader may become frustrated and start focusing on conditions, events, and people problems. He may better focus on how to organize their work or combine their work into an operating system in which the people are working together to achieve a planned outcome. In some church organizations there is fragmented work that could be organized into an existing system or organized into a new system that would save time and effort.

Possible short-term subsystems involving other systems within an organization may be needed to accomplish a short-term outcome and then terminated. Like the farmer, some leaders may see fragmented work to be done but do not see how to incorporate it into an existing system.

In order to keep a system functioning, it is important to calendar interviews with the leaders managing the systems to report on progress.

---

**Insight: The effective leader is never satisfied with the status quo.**

---

Until the leader begins to analyze and tries to determine the *cause* rather than focusing on the *effect,* he will continue to be an *event reactive* leader. Through a period of analyzing, the leader may determine the cause of poor work performance. The people may not have been taught or trained how to do their work effectively; therefore, they may need a system of training.

A program is a set of activities to accomplish a purpose. Programs come and go, and often give new direction that may or may not accomplish the purpose and vision of the organization. Proposing a new program is serious business and must be well thought out so that the program accomplishes the needs of the organization, not the needs of an existing program. If a program does not fit into an organizational system, then it may lack staying power. It may be best not to consider that new program.

Manage systems by determining major objectives that are to be achieved. Establish the end results to achieve the major objectives. Delegate responsibility in the form of specific expectations in order to achieve the objective. Establish a tracking method to follow up on achieving results and the expected objectives.

---

**Insight: Seeing and thinking is a prerequisite
for creating a system.**

---

**To turn on the power in your organization, influence leaders to (1) analyze, (2) organize, and (3) systematize.**

# THE POWER OF SYSTEMS

## Analyze
1. Are individuals encouraged to analyze how they can do better?
2. Are programs and activities analyzed to see if they accomplish the organization's purpose?
3. Do leaders effectively analyze current reality to determine what needs to be done?

## Organize
1. Have fragmented parts of the organization been organized into the whole?
2. Have work and time been organized for greater efficiency?
3. Are people organized to accomplish specific objectives and results?

## Systematize
1. Is the total organization effectively integrated to accomplish the purpose of the organization?
2. Have those parts of the organization that should be better systematized been determined?
3. Has a system been identified that could create greater efficiency?

# THE POWER TO GET THINGS DONE

"In the doing comes the power."
Ralph Waldo Emerson

When I go to the airport to catch a plane, I enjoy getting on the escalator, setting my luggage by my side, and riding along with the other people until it is time to get off. One day, while riding the escalator, I thought how it represented some organizations, moving along doing the same things the same way, day after day, and always arriving at the same outcome. I felt I was like some leaders that are being carried along horizontally by the momentum of the organization. Just as the escalator moved me along, some leaders, rather than leading, are moved along by the flow and happenings of the organization.

On another occasion, I took an elevator. When I walked into the elevator, I had to think about where I wanted to go. I had to know what I wanted to do and then push the right button to get there. My goal was to get off on the second floor. While riding to the second floor, I planned what I was going to do when I got off the elevator. As I got off the elevator, I checked to see if I had all my luggage and then proceeded to my objective.

The "escalator leader" is reactive. He is carried along by what is happening in the organization. His vision is mostly limited to his desk and to current problems. He spends time fulfilling current responsibilities and routine duties. These are all things that have to be done, but his leadership awareness suffers because he lacks vision beyond the organizational escalator on which he is riding. The people in his organization are moving horizontally with him, following his example with little awareness about future outcomes.

On the other hand the "elevator leader" is innovative. He is not only upbeat, but moving up. He sees the big picture and is aware of where he is going. He is creative, imaginative, resourceful, and positive. He sees, feels, delegates, and pushes the right buttons concerning what needs to be done. He thinks and plans for the future. He is continually concerned about moving the entire organization vertically, and that the people are following him.

Richard L Evans stated it effectively: "Sooner or later in life comes a time when it is performance that counts—not promises, not possibilities, not potentialities—but performance. Sooner or later there comes a time when sitting and watching are not enough—when doing something for ourselves and doing something for others is essential. It is good to sit and listen; it is good to sit and watch; it is good to sit and learn; but the law of improvement is the law of practice, of participation, of performance."

---

**Insight: The law of accomplishment is effectively achieving important outcomes.**

---

What people do or do not do depends a great deal on the ability of the leader to influence, inspire, and motivate them to achieve. An effective leader determines what needs to be done and selects the right people to do it. Being busy does not always achieve the right outcomes. Being busy without a purpose or vision is like treading water, doing something but not going anywhere. We must be busy doing important things and achieving important results. To achieve important objectives, you must:

**Effectively Manage the Big 3:**

# 1. COUNCILS
# 2. RESULTS
# 3. MINUTES

# ———COUNCILS———

Councils are usually composed of a leadership team linking operating units together. Councils provide an opportunity for group leaders to get together under a leader's direction to discuss, consult, listen, solve problems, make decisions, and receive direction. The sharing relationship of a council generates ideas and suggestions that benefit each unit and the total organization. Councils are one of the best ways to solve problems, create new outcomes, find the answer to specific concerns, overcome challenges, get important things done, and make a difference.

Elder M. Russell Ballard, in his excellent book *Counseling with Our Councils,* teaches the importance of Church councils when he quotes from the *Encyclopedia of Mormonism:* " 'As members participate in councils, they learn about larger organizational issues. They see leadership in action, learning how to plan, analyze problems, made decisions, and coordinate across subunit boundaries. Participation in councils helps prepare members for future leadership responsibilities'" ("Priesthood Councils," in Ludlow, *Encyclopedia of Mormonism* 3:1141-42; as cited in Ballard, p. 6).

The effective leader encourages each council member to listen and to contribute to the discussions. The leader seeks to achieve agreement on accomplishing a united outcome and then focuses on how to achieve that outcome. The inspired, effective leader uses a council to build tremendous organizational energy to get important things done.

**Common faults with councils are:**

1. **The leader has no planned agenda.**
2. **The focus is on problems and activities rather than on desired outcomes.**
3. **Things that matter most are at the mercy of things that matter least.**

**4. Time is spent discussing problems rather than solutions to problems.**
**5. Participants are not asked to achieve specific results.**

Councils coordinate the resources of all units to accomplish the purpose and vision of the organization. In a council setting, leaders have an opportunity to learn from and about each other as they share their knowledge, experiences, and resources about what needs to be done and how to do it. The leaders develop a cooperative relationship that encourages shared commitment concerning important issues and objectives.

Councils also have a great influence on establishing the values and culture of the organization. The effective leader uses councils to determine people and unit needs, receive suggestions for solutions to problems, obtain reports on previously assigned results, and delegate new results to be achieved.

---

**Insight: Councils determine leadership values and the culture of an organization**

---

The effective council leader keeps council members informed concerning:

1. *What* is happening.
2. *What* is expected.
3. *Why* it is expected.
4. *When* it is expected.
5. *Why* it is important.

Over years of observing "ho hum" council meetings, I have found that the biggest problem is the lack of a defined purpose and an agenda for the meeting. When there is no vision, and the leader holds a routine council meeting with no agenda, there may be a feeling of doing, but very few of the right things will get done When the purpose and vision of the organization is ingrained in the mind and memory of the leader, it becomes a compass that directs the thoughts, actions, and desired results of the council members.

The agenda is prepared in advance, containing the items to be discussed from council members. The leader monitors the discussion and ensures that all council members participate, which includes asking questions or soliciting comments from those least inclined to speak up. Periodically, he summarizes the discussions in concise language and finds a common ground for decisions. He then delegates assignments to achieve specific results. Purpose-directed council meetings are how effective leaders get important things done.

Routine, poorly planned council meetings often get out of control by allowing participants to just visit about items that are not pertinent to the agenda items or the discussion at hand, including hidden agenda items, favourite stories, or ego-building experiences. When this happens, the council meeting is run by those attending the meeting rather than by the leader of the meeting. A skilled leader focuses on receiving pertinent feedback on what has or has not been accomplished, guides the discussion toward achieving results, and determines what assignments to delegate. In this way, leaders overcome "ho hum" council meetings.

Watching a great football team perform precision plays is exciting. That happens when the coach holds effective meetings focussing on the purpose of the football team, which is to win. Think what would happen if a football coach held a meeting with no chalk talk, with team members talking about their own experiences, with no instructions about what is expected of each player, and without discussing important winning plays. Chaos and a losing team would result.

**To overcome "ho hum" council meetings:**

**1. Prepare a planned and shared agenda.**
**2. Follow up on previously delegated assignments.**
**3. Always start the meeting on time and end on time.**
**4. Mentally establish time periods for each agenda item.**
**5. See that decisions are reached, and expected results are assigned**

**and recorded.**

6. **Focus on accomplishing desired and needed outcomes.**
7. **Evaluate meeting performance. (Are desired outcomes accomplished?)**
8. **Ask and receive feedback for improvement, progress, and possibilities.**

One of Abraham Lincoln's cabinet members once invited him to come and listen to a great speaker. Lincoln went to hear the speaker. On their way back to the White House, the cabinet member asked Lincoln, "Wasn't that a great speech?" Lincoln answered, "Yes, except for one thing. He did not ask us to do anything." To overcome "ho hum" council meetings, get everyone to participate in the meeting, and help them anticipate accomplishing results by asking them to report on results progress during the next meeting.

Two methods previously mentioned that I have found help a leader limit unnecessary conversation and stick to the agenda, reducing meeting time. When people raise problems, listen to the problem and then ask, "What have you decided is a solution to the problem?" If they have no solution, invite them to think about a solution and place the item on the next agenda.

The second method I learned while attending a stake conference in Canada. We were in a meeting with the stake presidency, and someone opened the door and said to the stake president, "Sorry, President, but I have a serious problem." Then he stated the problem. The president asked, "What is your recommendation?" The man stopped talking, began thinking, and gave the president his recommendation. The president said, "That is good. Go ahead." Practice asking people, "What is your recommendation?"

I was very impressed how the president handled that situation. While in meetings or other situations when people present problems and concerns, ask the question what is your recommendation?" That question causes a person to think, conserves conversation, empowers people, and often creates a good solution to the problem. If there is no recommendation, suggest they think about it and then come back with a recommendation. These two questions—"Do you have a solution?" and "What is your recommendation?"—cause people to think, control their conversation, reduce meeting time, and get important things done.

The above principles could be called "**Don't Bring Me Problems, Bring Me Solutions.**"

> **Insight: Causing people to think, empowers people and the organization.**

An effective council is a united, motivated team of leaders who are of one heart and one mind and are committed to work together to achieve a common purpose.

**Key principles for building a united leadership council:**

1. **Members understand the purpose and work of the council.**
2. **Members know their individual assignments.**
3. **Members feel free to communicate with each other.**
4. **Members are all involved in the decision-making process.**
5. **Members' differences and conflicts are freely discussed.**
6. **Members are committed and motivated to make a difference in peoples' lives.**
7. **Members are achieving specific end results.**

## ————RESULTS————

When people in an organization have faith and confidence in their leader and their leader is inspired and result directed, the organization "stays alive." The organization stays alive when the people in the organization are also result directed. Results are achieved when people work in a result directed environment. It has been my experience in observing successful leaders and organizations that results are achieved when the following three conditions exist:

**1. Result directed leaders.**
**2. Result directed people.**
**3. Result directed environment.**

A result directed leader has a clear understanding of the purpose and vision of the organization. He realizes that he is never alone in the work of the Lord. Through his prayers and righteous desires, he charts the course and initiates the action within the organization. He is involved in creating a result directed environment by delegating specific results to be achieved and by expecting people to achieve those results. He see that individuals are rewarded for their efforts with the proper recognition. He thinks about the here and now and is also focussed enough on the future to anticipate future trends, changes, and possibilities.

Result directed people in an organization are important in overcoming inertia within the organization and also within the mind and heart of the people. Result directed people become proactive rather than reactive. Their energies are focused on achieving rather than on grieving that things are not done.

A result directed environment requires a result directed leader. Such a leader is aware that it is the combined efforts of the people in the organization that achieve the desired outcome. When the people in the organization become accustomed to achieving end results, they become accustomed to thinking in terms of how to achieve the end results and create a result directed environment.

## ———MINUTES———

Minutes of a meeting are brief notes detailing the proceedings of the meeting. Minutes are a written record the discussion, decisions, assignments, and actions taken in order to accomplish desired outcomes. Effectively written and recorded minutes influence the purpose and vision of the organization and the performance of the people in the organization. *Minutes influence the organization.*

Minutes are a resource to answering questions about problems, agreeing on policy, clearing up conflicts, and keeping people on track and informed. While I was serving as secretary to the Quorum of the Twelve, past minutes were regularly called for to help maintain consistency of policy and to review past decisions, standards, and arguments previously agreed upon, and information helpful to making current decisions. Minutes are the memory of the leadership council.

**The leader helps to formulate good minutes by:**

1. **Asking questions to determine understanding.**
2. **Summarizing conversation.**
3. **Seeking agreement on what action should be taken.**
4. **Indicating who is assigned to achieve the desired results.**

Minutes become a good follow-up tool. If an action item has been delegated, note the person who is assigned the item. The first items on the next meeting agenda should be "follow-up items" from the previous meeting. The "return and report" principle is an important reason for keeping accurate minutes. Maintaining complete and accurate minutes preserves organizational integrity and leadership effectiveness.

## SUGGESTIONS FOR GETTING THINGS DONE

### Think

Your mind must take the lead! Right thinking brings right results. We tend to become what we think about. If you want to achieve something, think about it. The mental law is "cause and effect." Our thoughts are the cause, and the actions and consequences are the effect. You will achieve what you think about. Determine your objectives, mentally focus on them, and you will achieve them.

**Answer Yes to the Following Questions?**

1. Have you determined desired outcomes?
2. Are you monitoring expected progress?
3. Are you maintaining a list of things that need to be done?
4. Have you delegated specific results to be accomplished?
5. Are you continually asking yourself, "Are we going where we want to go?"

**Write Your Annual Achievement Plan**

1. Know where your organization is now.
2. Know where you want to go.
3. Identify specific objectives to be achieved.
4. Determine how the objectives will be achieved.
5. Identify a few critical measurements to judge your progress and success.

**Problem Solving**

*First*, clearly define the problem. Defining the problem solves about 50 percent of the problem.
*Second*, collect information. Get the facts or the facts will get you.
*Third*, ask for advice. Learn from the experience of others.
*Fourth*, think and ponder concerning the problem and the information you have gathered. If you don't have to rush into an answer, sleep on it. Keep in mind that the answer that comes at 4:30 in the morning, if not written down, may not be available at breakfast time. Keep a pad and pencil at your bedside.

## THE 10–20 PRINCIPLE

Brainstorming is a great way to obtain new and different ideas for solving problems, fulfilling challenges, and answering concerns. Use the 10–20 principle. This method encourages you, or a group, to come up with 10 to 20 ideas about how to solve a problem, concern, or challenge. You may find that ideas 8, 9, and 10 or items 18, 19, and 20 are your best ideas. The first few ideas are the common and easy ones that people will come up with. The last items are usually the very best, because they come from deep thinking.

## Focus on Accomplishing Goals; Keep in Mind Your G.P.A.

**1. G,** goals, the end results to be achieved.
**2. P,** point, focussing on the goal.
**3. A,** action, making the decision to act.
Focus on keeping a high G. P. A. in your organization.

## Do One Job at a Time

Do not jump from one job to another. Stay with the current task until it is completed. Successful people carry out tasks to completion. When you have more than you feel you can do, stop complaining and start thinking how to do it. Prioritize, organize, simplify, or delegate to determine how conditions can be changed so you can do it.

## Make Time to Read

Have reading material always available to read at home, car, travelling, etc. A reader may not be a leader, but a leader is always a reader.

## Write It Down

Keep 3x5 cards, notebook or planner available to write things down. When something comes to your mind that has to be done, write it down, A short pencil is better than a long memory.

## Task Committees

A task committee is a group of six to eight people who the leader has assigned to meet together one or two times to discuss a specific problem and come up with specific recommendation for the leader to consider.

## Be a Flexible Leader

Leaders who are flexible are better qualified to overcome problems and challenging situations because they are willing to explore alternative options. They have the ability to "roll with life's punches." Blessed are the flexible, they don't get bent out of shape.

## Do not Procrastinate

Procrastination is a bad habit, a habit that is hard to break. A procrastinator is a lazy thinker whose motivation is stifled by lack of self discipline. His success is limited until he overcomes the habit of procrastination. Busy people do not have time to procrastinate.

## Be an Effective Follower

President Joseph F. Smith taught: "Every man should be willing to be presided over, and he is not fit to preside over others until he can submit sufficiently to the presidency of his brethren" (*Improvement Era,* 17 Dec. 1917, p. 105).

**Effectively manage the Big 3—(1) Councils, (2) Results, and (3) Minutes—and you will turn on the power in your organization.**

# THE POWER TO GET THINGS DONE

|  | Need Improvement | Satisfactory | Very Good |
|---|---|---|---|

**Leadership**

1. Leaders focus on achieving important outcomes? _____ _____ _____
2. Reactive leaders are being trained to be proactive? _____ _____ _____
3. Most leaders are innovative and result directed? _____ _____ _____

**Council Meetings**

1. Members work from an agenda? _____ _____ _____
2. Leaders ask for recommendations & solutions? _____ _____ _____
3. Members feel free to present their ideas? _____ _____ _____
4. Meetings start and end on time? _____ _____ _____

**Results**

1. Result directed meetings are held? _____ _____ _____
2. Members have a result directed attitude _____ _____ _____
3. Members are assigned specific results to achieve? _____ _____ _____

**Minutes**

1. Minutes are concise, stating conclusions and decisions? _____ _____ _____
2. Action items are delegated? _____ _____ _____
3. Action items are recorded and followed up on? _____ _____ _____
4. Minutes are read and approved? _____ _____ _____

# THE POWER TO GET THINGS DONE

|  | Need Improve-ment | Satisfactory | Very Good |
|---|---|---|---|
| **Leadership** | | | |
| 1. Leaders focus on achieving important outcomes? | _____ | _____ | _____ |
| 2. Reactive leaders are being trained to be proactive? | _____ | _____ | _____ |
| 3. Most leaders are innovative and result directed? | _____ | _____ | _____ |
| **Council Meetings** | | | |
| 1. Members work from an agenda? | _____ | _____ | _____ |
| 2. Leaders ask for recommendations & solutions? | _____ | _____ | _____ |
| 3. Members feel free to present their ideas? | _____ | _____ | _____ |
| 4. Meetings start and end on time? | _____ | _____ | _____ |
| **Results** | | | |
| 1. Result directed meetings are held? | _____ | _____ | _____ |
| 2. Members have a result directed attitude | _____ | _____ | _____ |
| 3. Members are assigned specific results to achieve? | _____ | _____ | _____ |
| **Minutes** | | | |
| 1. Minutes are concise, stating conclusions and decisions? | _____ | _____ | _____ |
| 2. Action items are delegated? | _____ | _____ | _____ |
| 3. Action items are recorded and followed up on? | _____ | _____ | _____ |
| 4. Minutes are read and approved? | _____ | _____ | _____ |

# THE POWER OF CHARACTER

"Our master is absent only a little season,
and at the end of it he will call each to render an account"
(Joseph Smith, *Teachings of the Prophet Joseph Smith*, p. 68).

A basic principle of life is that right action is a prerequisite to receiving inner strength. This is true of both building physical muscles and moral character. To deny that which corrupts for that which is ethical, honorable, and good develops character. Effort in resisting temptation strengthens the mind and spirit and develops the will power to do what is right and good.

The righteous leader is always evaluating his performance according to the teachings of the scriptures, prophets, and inner guidance. He realizes that if he magnifies his calling and is honest and worthy in every respect, the Lord will inspire him and magnify him before the people he serves.

A person remains at the level on which his mind dwells. As long as a person's mind dwells and remains on the level of lower primitive impulses and materialistic enticements, he may wallow in an element of depravity, and mediocrity. Our thoughts and actions must reach for a much higher spiritual level to develop the power of character.

The power of character comes from commitment to righteous principles. Conform your life to what you know is right and true, and you will build your character and influence others.

"Every great institution is the lengthened shadow of a single man,
His character determines the character of the organization."
Ralph Waldo Emerson

---

**Insight: Organizations are energized by light and truth.**

---

**Three pillars of character are:**

# 1. PERSONAL INTEGRITY
# 2. HONORABLE VALUES AND BELIEFS
# 3. RIGHTEOUS INFLUENCE

## ———PERSONAL INTEGRITY———

---

**Insight: The essence of a sterling reputation
is personal integrity.**

---

Personal integrity is the power to be honorable, honest, and incorruptible. Integrity is not something that is automatic. It is achieved by overcoming temptation, the corruptions of the world, and the evils of our environment through "right effort." Integrity is the result of moral self-discipline leading to self-mastery and self-improvement.

The great challenge of this day is to maintain personal integrity in a world where there is so much dishonesty, immoral enticements, and low personal standards of behavior in a world where there is lewdness and corruption.

President Dwight Eisenhower said: "In order to be a leader, a man must have followers. And to have followers, a man must have their confidence. Hence, the superman quality for a leader is unquestionably integrity. Without it, no real success is possible, no matter whether it is on a section gang, a football field, in an army, or in an office. If a man's associates find him guilty of being a phony, if they find that he lacks forthright integrity, he will fail. His teachings and actions must square with each other. The first great need, therefore, is integrity and high purpose" (*Great Quotes from Great Leaders,* ed. Peggy Anderson).

While living in an environment in which there is much dishonesty, some people may think it futile to live a life of personal integrity. However, the alternative is to fall into the sewer of corruption, immorality, and deviant behavior and ultimately to lose self-respect and the respect of others.

Personal integrity and moral strength come when we care enough to be involved in helping others to be right, honest, and truthful. By working to overcome evil, helping others to oppose evil, and striving to do what is right, we escape much heartache, suffering, and despair. To develop our character is to obey our conscience and progress continually toward inner peace and happiness.

If we are personally responsible for doing something we know to be spiritually illegal and contrary to our moral values, we will suffer spiritual pain. Nothing less than confession, repentance, and renewed personal integrity can restore our inner peace. I have known leaders who restored their sense of personal integrity and regained inner peace because they were willing to accept and live the following steps:

1. **Accept full responsibility for a dishonorable act through repentance.**
2. **Commit to change.**
3. **Acknowledge to the relevant person or persons the harm you have done.**
4. **Make restitution as far as possible.**
5. **Strongly commit yourself to act honorably and righteously in the future.**

Without these steps, a person may continue to feel the pain of guilt caused by dishonorable behavior and may not be relieved of his or her pain. If we do what is right and appropriate, the feeling of guilt will disappear. Our honor and integrity will be restored.

Be honest and truthful. Take responsibility for your choices and your behavior. Follow the precepts of the Golden Rule, "Do unto others as you would have others do unto you," and enjoy inner peace and help enjoy social tranquility.

# ——HONORABLE VALUES AND BELIEFS——

Men and women possessing honorable and righteous values will have the power to teach true principles and to be able to inspire and influence people positively. A leader who has internalized righteous beliefs and is governed by righteous values has a powerful influence upon those with whom he works. Such a leader has a good name and is respected by all that work with him or her.

> **Insight: People's values and beliefs give life and strength to an organization.**

I am reminded of a story I heard about a very wise man. In the city of Kathmandu, Nepal, there lived a wise man. People from Nepal and India went to him for counsel and advice. He spoke freely to the people, asking for nothing in return. A young man who had spent and lost his money approached him and asked, "What shall I do to receive the most for what I spend?" The wise man said, "Anything bought or sold has no value unless it contains that which cannot be bought or sold. Look for the Priceless Ingredient." "But what is this Priceless Ingredient?" asked the young man. The wise man then said, "My son, the Priceless Ingredient of every product in the marketplace is the honor and integrity of him who makes it or sells it. Consider his name before you buy."

A person who values his or her name values the moral principles and beliefs that govern his or her thinking and actions.

Daily we face conflicting feelings and desires. We struggle with situations that demand choices. Honorable values establish rules of conduct and standards for resolving conflicts and for making right decisions. Honorable values unite the mind, body, and spirit in making proper choices in a world of conflicting alternatives.

Sydney Newton Bremer explained some of the challenges we face that establish the need for guiding values: "At each moment of a man's life he is either a king or a slave. As he surrenders to wrong appetite, to any human weaknesses, as he falls prostrate in hopeless subjection to any condition, to any environment, to failure, he is a slave. As he day by day crushes out human weaknesses, masters opposing elements within him, and day by day recreates a new self from the sin and folly of his past—he is a king" (*How to Get What You Want* [Successful Achievement], 126).

Values and beliefs provide a standard for people to make right decisions and for leaders to formulate "right policies" and give "right direction."

**Righteous values and beliefs endow the organization with:**

**1. Moral principles.**
**2. Beliefs that govern action.**
**3. Standards of conduct.**
**4. Trustful relationships.**

Peter Drucker said: "'Trust is the conviction that the leader means what he says. It is a belief in something very old-fashioned called integrity.' A leader's actions and a leader's professed beliefs must be congruent or at least compatible. Effective leadership—and again this is very old wisdom— not based on being clever; it is based primarily on being consistent" (*Management, Tasks, Responsibilities and Practices*).

**Influential leaders value and believe in:**

**1. Being an example—consistent in righteous behavior.**
**2. Being approachable—open and receptive.**
**3. Being teachable—willing to learn.**
**4. Being prayerful—spiritually in tune.**

# ———RIGHTEOUS INFLUENCE———

In the doing comes the power. A leader who uses his agency to conduct his life according to divine law develops the power to live divine law. He enjoys the positive consequences of right behavior and an exemplary character.

Influence is earned from the people with whom we work. A leader will not have influence with people until he has proven himself worthy of their respect and support. A successful leader understands that he is allowed by others to influence their thinking, attitudes, and actions only if he or she is worthy and respected.

Influence implies that the leader is accepted and is looked to for guidance and direction. He or she is perceived as capable, productive, sensitive, and helpful. The influential leader realizes that people are the portals through which men and women pass into positions of power and greatness.

---

**Insight: Character and influence are prerequisites to greatness.**

---

## BEATITUDES OF INFLUENCE

*Be considerate, courteous, and kind to others.*
*Be dependable, reliable, and responsible in your work.*
*Be consistent, cooperative, and supportive in your behavior.*
*Be invaluable, indispensable, and essential to the organization.*
Author unknown

Influence has a great deal to do with our relationship with people. People who are liked and honorable will have a positive influence upon people. We all have our good conduct and our not so good conduct.

Improving our conduct or behavior will improve our influence with people.

**To improve your behavior:**

**1. Recognize your not so good behavior. (If you do not recognize it, you cannot change it.)**
**2. Desire to overcome your not so good behavior. (Desire creates the power to do.)**
**3. Affirm your new behavior. (Think, affirm, and see your new behavior daily.)**
**4. Practice your new behavior. (Practice until your new behavior becomes a habit.)**

Helping others to grow, improve, and succeed is a product of leadership, character, and influence. People, not organizations, get things done and accomplish results. A person of influence will continually be mindful of Thomas Carlyle's statement:

*"The ideal is in thyself. The impediment, too, is in thyself."*

Persons who challenge themselves to overcome impediments and seek to achieve the ideal will maintain a positive influence with others. The power to influence people is created by a leader's personal values, worthiness, and integrity. A person of character does what he says he will do, when he says he will do it, and according to predetermined standards.

Only to the degree that we are true to ourselves and our values and are continually learning, helping, and encouraging others to grow and improve, will we have the power of positive influence. Our communications should always be with love and kindly persuasion, giving others the opportunity to discuss their feelings while listening with real intent. Influence is developed as we become more sensitive to other's needs.

Peter Drucker defined *efficiency* as "doing things right" versus *effectiveness* "doing the right things." We can be very efficient in doing things, but to be a leader of influence we must become effective in doing the right things right. We develop self-perfection by doing all things in a righteous manner. Whatever action we perform, that action has consequences.

Two frogs lived in a pool. The pool dried up during the warm weather. They left their pool to seek a better home. As they were looking, one frog noticed a deep well filled with water. The frog said, "Let us go down and live in the well." The other replied with concern, "What if the well dried up? How would we get out of the well?" The moral of this story is to be cautious and alert until you determine the future consequences of your actions. Perform right action, and you will receive the fruits of right action. Perform wrong action, and you will receive the fruits of wrong action. It is the law of the harvest

Character building activities include learning, reading, and growing. It is keeping commitments, covenants, and commandments. An important part of character building and your personal progress comes through doing what is necessary in order to be magnified before the people you serve. If you neglect your duty to self, others, and your work, your conscience will create an inner, unsettled feeling. How you respond to that feeling greatly determines your character, consequences, experiences, and destiny.

> Sow a thought, and you reap an act;
> Sow an act, and you reap a habit;
> Sow a habit, and you reap a character;
> Sow a character, and you reap a destiny.

Ralph Waldo Emerson

# I AM TRUE TO MYSELF

I have to live with myself, and so
I want to be fit for myself to know.
I want to be able, as days go by,
Always to look myself straight in the eye;
I don't want to stand, with the setting sun,
And hate myself for things I have done.
I don't want to keep on a closet shelf
A lot of secrets about myself
And fool myself, as I come and go,
Into thinking that nobody else will know
The kind of man I really am;
I don't want to dress up myself in sham.
I want to go out with my head erect,
I want to deserve all men's respect;
But here in the struggle for fame and pelf
I want to be able to like myself.
I don't want to look at myself and know
That I'm bluster and bluff and empty show.
I can never hide myself from me;
I see what others may never see;
I know what others may never know.
I can never fool myself, and so,
Whatever happens, I want to be
Self-respecting and conscience free.

Edgar Guest

**Righteous leadership includes (1) personal integrity, (2) honorable values, and (3) righteous influence, all of which are necessary to turn on the power to achieve desired outcomes in your organization.**

# THE POWER OF CHARACTER

## INTEGRITY
1. I am honest in dealing with other people.
2. I encourage things to be done in a right, honest, and truthful way.
3. I place honesty before achievement and recognition.


## VALUES
1. My values show in my performance.
2. My decisions and actions are in harmony with my values.
3. My values influence how I treat others.


## INFLUENCE
1. I am a positive influence on people with whom I work.
2. I strive to influence others to grow and do what is right.
3. I model and expect right behavior.

# REVIEW

## THE POWER OF LEADERSHIP

Achievement with people is built on a foundation of effective leadership. Successful achievement is the result of successful leadership, which is built on a foundation of:

1. **Credibility:** Inspires, motivates, and achieves.
2. **Social Ability:** Creates friendship, stewardship, and followership.
3. **Communications Ability:** Inspires, motivates, and achieves right outcomes.

## THE POWER OF VISION

Vision is the power to see what needs be achieved in the future. It is the energy to overcome problems, challenges, and a guide to success.

1. **Perform A Critical Analysis:** What you see is what you get.
2. **Set Direction:** Constancy of direction creates constancy of results.
3. **Communicate Expectations:** Results, possibilities and opportunities.

## THE POWER OF FOCUSING

An important part of being successful is determining what is most important to achieve and then determining how and when to achieve it.

1. **Focus on Achieving End Results:** Right results achieves right objectives.
2. **Focus on Sustained Attention:** What holds attention determines action.
3. **Focus on Purposeful action:** What gets measured gets done.

## THE POWER OF PLANNING

If people and your organization are growing, changing, and progressing, you are planning. Planning makes the difference.

1. **Planning Future Direction:** Creating a successful future requires planning.
2. **Planning Right Outcomes:** Give purpose, credibility, and direction to our lives.
3. **Planning for Success:** Planners are movers, doers, and achievers..

## THE POWER OF EFFECTIVE OPERATIONS

Operating units operate as an integral part of the total organization. The proactive leader will always take time to critically analyze how each operating unit is achieving its purpose and vision.

1. **Monitoring People Performance:** Doing the same things brings the same results.
2. **Guiding Operational Units:** Communicate what you expect and when you expect it.
3. **Follow Up on Expected Results:** People will rise to the expectations of their leader.

## THE POWER OF MOTIVATION

To motivate others, a leader must first be self-motivated. People are willing to follow a committed and motivated leader.

1. **Self-Motivation:** Successful people do what failures don't like to do.
2. **People Motivation:** Effective leaders create a happy, positive, and rewarding environment.
3. **Organizational Motivation:** You receive the same kind of behavior that you reward.

## THE POWER OF SYSTEMS

A system starts first with identifying needs and organizing those needs into existing systems or creating a new system.

**1. Analyze:** Analyzing is a prerequisite to organizing and systemizing.
**2. Organize:** To accomplish objectives and desired outcomes.
**3. Systemize:** Systems have the ability to maintain themselves.

## THE POWER TO GET THINGS DONE

What people do or don't do depends a great deal on the ability of the leader to influence, inspire, motivate, and lead people to get the important thing done.

**1. Councils:** Inspire and coordinate organizational units to successful achievement.
**2. Results:** Influence result-leaders, result-environments, and result-people.
**3. Minutes:** Clear, specific, and correct minutes will influence the organization.

## THE POWER OF CHARACTER

Organizations are energized by the character and dedication of an inspiring leader.

**1. Personal Integrity:** To be found lacking, the leader fails.
**2. Honorable Values:** Values are the mortar of an organization.
**3. Righteous Influence:** Influence is earned when a leader is worthy of respect.

# INDEX

abilities, to more effectively accomplish, 33; to influence others, 6

ability, 1; to lead successfully, 2; to inspire confidence, 3; to listen, 8; to sense, 8; to persuade others, 14; to contribute, 17; to envision the future, 26; to manage yourself, 60

Abraham, 55

Abraham Lincoln, 4

accept responsibility, 54

accommodate, 77

accomplish, expected objectives, 22; 36; new outcomes, 49

accomplishing, your vision, 16; results, 25, 86; goals, 40

accomplishment, law of, 82

achieve, results, 6; generalities, 28; what you focus on, 28; desired results, 41; the objectives, 43; desired outcome, 56; your expectations, 56; the expected results, 82; 89; 101

achievement, 22, 27; motivation for, 37; plan, 43; and improvement, 64; price for, 65; 104, 105

achievements, 39

achievers are planners, 42

achieving, 2; ability, 11; new results, 16; the purpose of the organization, 19; 21; future objectives, 22; power, 23; 25; focus on, 26; desired results, 23, leaders, 26; 29; improvement, 29; power, 30,

33; end results, 33; climate, 42; results, 48, 49, 54; the expectations, 58; person, 64; 71; results, 79; 82; 85; 87; 106

acting, 2

action, 31; 75

action-compelling possibilities, 19

actions speak louder, 3

active leader, 48

activities and programs, 16

activity fat, 17

adaptability, 41

administrative work, 29

agency, 100

agenda, 56; 85

alcohol, 4

alert and focused, 30

alternative options, 92

analyze, 19, 74, 76, 79, 80, 107

annual achievement plan, 90

anxiously engaged, 30

appreciated, 6

appreciation builds success, 55

appreciation, 51, 57, 58, 69

approachable, 6. 9

appropriate action, 47

appropriate motivation, 59

art of multiplying yourself, 45

atrophy and stagnate, 21

attainable objectives, 48

attendance, 5

attention, 4; to the organizational flow, 29; to achieving, 29

attitude(s), 37, 39; mindful of, 48; of venture, 49; 93

availability, 1

awareness, 48

balance, 29
Ballard, M. Russell, 83
basic principles, of leadership, 5;
    of effective training, 67
beatitudes of influence, 100
behavior, 101, 106
believability, 3
believe and achieve, 33
believing and achieving, 21
benefits for taking action, 31
Benson, Ezra Taft, 1, 38, 45
bishop, major responsibility of, 36
bishops, 32
blueprint for accomplishing, 36
bonding happens, 56
brainstorm, 34
brainstorming, 90
build commitment, 20
building friendships, 6
busy work, 16

calendaring, 56
call to influence the future, 15
call to leadership, 15
called by prophecy, 2
calling, magnifying their, 5
callings, happy in their, 21
calmness of mind, 69
capability, 1
capable, 100
casual conversation, 8, 9, 31
cause and effect, 89
cautious risks, 49
cautious discussion, 8
center of attention, 76
center of power, 59
challenges, 14, 16, 18, 36, 60
challenging leadership styles, 7
challenging children, 50
chance, 55
chaos, 85

character building activities, 102
character, person of, 101
character, power of, 95
character traits, 4
Church callings, 25
Church councils, 83
Church, mission of the, 21, 49, 68-69
clear and measurable standards, 28
clear expectations, 23
clear objectives, 68
clear picture of future results, 22
clear sentences, 9
clerks, 56
climate for achieving, 9
climate of trust, 6
collective behavior, 47
collective energy, 25
colorless, 7
comfort zone, 2
comfortable and secure, 6
commandments, 102
commit, 31
commitment, 15; 50; to the
    purpose, 58; 84; 95
commitments, 102
communicate, 9; clearly, 12;
    expectations, 16, 21, 23; the
    plan, 43; 52; with
    understanding, 56
communication, 70
communicating ability, 2, 7, 10,
    12, 105
communicating, course in, 2
communicating results, 12
communication skills, 7-8
communications ability, 105
compelling organizational vision,
    22
compelling vision, 14-15, 18, 23
competence of the organization,

competency, 3
complacency, 41
complacency, the enemy of achievement, 64
completed results, 17
completion dates, 54
compliments, 12
concentrated energies, 25
concentration of effort, 25
concern for others, 12
concerned for other people, 6
conduct, standards of, 99
confession, 97
confidence, 55, 69, 87
conflicting alternatives, 98
conflicting opinions, 30
confusion, 77
conscience, 97, 102
consistency in direction, 58
consistency of action, 68
consistency of performance, 4
contention, 50
continual follow up, 55
control stifles motivation, 29
controlling, 29
conversation to enlighten, 8
conversation to the extreme, 7
cooperative, 22
cooperative associations with people, 6
corrective suggestions, 32
corruption, sewer of, 97
council meetings, 84-85, 93
councils, 81, 82, 92, 107
counsel from others, 8
counseling, 50
courage, 73
courage zone, 2
course corrections, 51
courteous, 100

courtesy, 72
covenants, 60, 102
create your credibility, 4; positive and supportive relationships, 6; understanding, 8
creating, credibility, 3, 12; more opportunities, 16; the vision of the organization, 18, 20; a motivating vision, 19
creation of the earth, 55
creative and innovative thinking, 37; creative thinking, 49
creativity and flexibility, 41
credibility, 2; people follow, 3; major creator of, 4; greatest influence, 5; strive to improve, 10; 12, 106
crisis management, 37
critical measurements, 90
critical analysis, 16; of your organization, 19; 23, 105
cross-purposes, 30
crucial information, 8
current reality, 22
currents of the organization, 29
currents of organizational pressures, 35
cycle of solving problems, 49

daily motivating power, 18
day dreaming, 22
deadline for achieving, 26
dedication, 68; and commitment, 22
defensive leader, 7-8
delegate, to others, 51; easy to, 54; 55, 75, 79, 91
delegated, assignments, 31, 55; action items, 56
delegating, end results, 29; 63, 88
delegation, 54

dependability, 1
dependable, 100
depravity, 95
desire, and willingness, 64; for
    greater achievement, 65; 70,
    101
desired major objectives, 16
desired movement, 21
desired objectives, 43
desired outcome(s), 2, 16, 22, 35,
    29; of the leaders, 32; 36-37,
    43, 47, 56, 78, 83, 90, 103
desired pre-determined outcome,
    36
desired results, 23, 28-29, 41; of
    the leader, 66; 89
desires, and ambitions, 39; 71
despair, 97
destination in mind, 35
destiny, 102
destroying influence, 4
detailed plan, 35
determine the strengths, 18
determined objectives, 47
determined the vital signs, 18
determining, your vision, 14;
    results, 29; direction, 36;
deviant behavior, 97
different approaches, 27
different leader, 7
different outcomes, 49
difficult to relate, 6
difficulties, 14
diligence, 52
diligent prayer, 23
diminishing, 4
direct leadership, 25
direct people's energy, 7
directing your efforts, 33
direction, and character, 13; sense
    of, 15; to the future, 16; for

the people, 19; of the
    organization, 20; 23, 28, 37,
    45, 83, 100, constancy of, 105;
    106
discernment, power of, 61
discontent with current reality, 22
dishonest men and women, 3
dishonesty, 97
dishonorable behavior, 97
disposition, 6
dispositions of people, 48
divine, inspiration, 48; guidance,
    60; law, 100
doctrine, 71
doctrine of welfare, 66
doing, 2; your duty, 5; but not
    achieving, 17; 29
domestic chores and duties, 21
dream(s) of a leader, 14; a dream,
    26; to be accomplished, 32;
    41, 71
Drucker, Peter, 14, 46
duty, 5, 52; to self, 102

earned abilities, 4
effective achievers, 72
effective follower, 92
effective communications, 7
effective communicator, 8
effective council, 87
effective council leader, 84
effective follow up, 55
effective in communicating
    results, 12
effective leader(s), 2, 6, 10, 21,
    26, 31, 35-37, 47, 54, 70, 78,
    83, 85
effective leaders listen, 8
effective leadership, 1, 9, 99
effective management, 45
effective methods of follow up, 56

effective operations, 48; 52; power
of, 57, 106
effective problem solving, 52
effective social ability, 6
effective stake president, 27
effective teachers, 10
effectively accomplish, 33
effectiveness, 6; 54; of the people,
55; 102
effectual attitude, 6
efficiency, 4, 80, 102
effort, concentration of, 25
effort, time, and discipline, 65
efforts to purposeful action, 33
ego-building experiences, 85
Einstein, Albert, 31
elevator leader, 82
Emerson, Ralph Waldo, 71, 73,
81, 95
emotion, 6
emotional, appeal, 28; energy, 9
emotional survival, 42
empower, 2, 17, 51
encourage people, 20
encouragement, 57, 71
end results, 105
enemies of progress, 22
energy of the sun rays, 25
energy, 32; to the organization, 33
enlarge or expand your calling, 5
enthusiasm, spirit of, 42
escalator leader, 81
establish follow-up procedures, 57
establish guide lines, 55
establishing major objectives, 36
eternal life of man, 13
evaluate, 49, 86
Evans, Richard L., 82
event reactive leader, 78
evil, overcoming, 97
example, 99; of most mothers, 54

excess fat in the organization, 16
excite your imagination, 65
excitement to achieve, 22
excitement, 20-21
exemplary character, 100
existing behavior, 59
existing non-productive
conditions, 49
expect, 65, 66
expectation(s), 20; clearly present,
21; 46, 52, 56, 105
expected actions, 32
expected results, 19
expected objectives, 22, 79
expected outcomes, 47-48
expected progress, 90
expected results, 28, 31, 42, 46,
53, 56-57, 85, 106
explain your expectations, 21
explaining stirs progress, 55
express praise, 12
expression, 6
extra mile, 42

fact-finding questions, 18
failure, 6, 35
failure points, 37
fairness in decisions, 68
faith, 2; a principle of action, 5; in
people, 7; to achieve, 14; 30;
and accomplishment, 31; 37;
in people, 66
faithful service, 5
family home evening, 21
fast with a purpose, 61
favorable response, 21
fear of reprimand, 55
feedback, 86
feedback information, 32
feeling(s) of the people, 8; and
attitudes, 17; and needs, 29;

of faith, 31; mindful of, 48
file leader(s), 1-2, 32, 51-52,
    chastised by, 54; 63
fire of achievement, 25
firm commitment, 4
First Presidency, 31
fix or modify existing conditions,
    16
flexibility of performance, 41
flexible leader, 92
focus, 2, 5; on achieving results, 9;
    on right outcomes, 18; on the
    opportunities, 20; on
    achieving, 26, 28; on
    spending, 29; on new
    approaches, 32; areas of, 36;
    65-66, 86, 91, 93
focused and directed, 32
focused direction, 25, 27
focused in the right direction, 29
focused leaders, 25, 30
focused on achieving expected
    results, 66
focusing, 9; the ability, 25; 32-33;
    power of, 34, 105; on the
    present, 37; 61
follow the example, 54
follow the prompting of the Spirit,
    5
follow through, 54, 65-66
follow-up artists, 53
follow up, on assignments, 10;
    reminders, 21; not so easy, 54;
    methods of, 55; time to, 56;
    procedures, 57; 89
following up on expected results,
    57
followship, course in 1; key
    elements of, 2
force that guides and pushes, 14
form of ideas, 23

formula for success, 22
freedom of expression and
    emotion, 6; of communication,
    12; spirit of, 42; to
    experiment, 54; to try new
    things, 55
friendliness, 12
frustration, 75, 77
full purpose of heart, 23
future accomplishments, 71
future achievements, 37, 41
future, best way to predict, 22
future direction, 36, 42, 106
future expectations, 39
future objectives, 22, 23
future opportunities, 14, 15, 18,
    28, 33
future possibilities for achieving,
    16
future trends, 88
fuzzy thinking, 22

Gandhi, 3
genius, 28
give recognition, 59
goal directed, 59
goals, 39, 70-71, 91
godhood, 38
Gods, 55
Goethe, 20
Golden Rule, 98
good behavior, 101
good conduct, 100
good communication, 69
good communicator, 9
good counsel, 38
good example of credibility, 3
good feedback, 32
good habit of self-motivation, 64
good leader, 2
good listener, 12

GPA, 91
grace, 2
grand wishes, 24
gratitude, 51, 58
great achievements, 41
great achievers, 41
great excitement, 21
great influence, 6
great leaders, 14
greater achievement, 65
greater desire, 17
greater influence, 35
greater inspiration, 64
greater power of discernment, 61
greater vision, 13
greatest genius, 20
greatest motivation principle, 63
greatest obstacles, 10
greatness, prerequisites to, 100
grieving, 88
group of bishops, 32
growing, 1, 102
growth, and progress, 55, 70
guidance, 100
guide operational units, 57
guidelines to follow, 38
guiding operational units, 46, 49
guiding vision, 13
guilt, pain of, 97

habit of procrastination, 64
happiness, 97
happy, 6
hard work, 37
hearts of the people, 20
heat energy, 25
help people, 55
help of others, 9
helpful, 100
helping others, to grow, 12; 97
helping people, 22, 30

hidden agenda, 85
high purpose, 97
higher spiritual level, 95
Hinckley, Gordon B., vision of, 15
Holy Spirit, power of, 23
Holy Spirit, voice of the, 64
home teaching, 31
honest, 104
Honest Abe, 4
honesty, 4
honor, 2; and integrity, 97
honorable values, 98, 103, 107
human body, 47
human behavior, 59
humble, 2
humor and positive comments, 7

ideas, and suggestions, 17; 31
identified concerns, 18
IEFF method, 65
immorality, 13, 97
important objectives, 25, 34, 36,
    39, 42, 82
important opportunities, 17
important responsibility, 55
important results, 30
important tasks, 55
important vital signs, 20
improve people, 19
improve people's credibility, 10
improve your communicating
    ability, 11
improved outcomes, 48
improvement and achievement, 49
improvement awareness, 48
improvement, law of, 82; 86
improving work, 29
inability, 33
inadequacies, 2
increase your social ability, 11
increased wisdom, 61

incredible power, 4
India, family in, 3
indispensable, 100
individual growth, 23
individual motivations, 60
individuality, 59
individuals in the organization, 39
inflexibility, 8
influence, to empower others, 3; 4,
    relationships, 10; on behavior,
    20, 35; 82, 104, 107;
    beatitudes of, 100; person of,
    101
influencing people, 1, 7
influential leader, 3
information gained, 19
initiative to achieve, 49
inner confidence, 6
inner guidance, 95
inner happiness, 69
inner peace, 4, 97-98
inner promptings, 23
inner self, 6
inner trauma, 4
innovative leadership, 41
innovative thinking, 37, 49
inquiring mind, 23
inspiration, 2, regarding new
    ideas, 19; 23; in overcoming,
    49; 64
inspired ability, 8
inspired conversation, 3
inspired programs of the Church,
    17
integrity, 4,96, 104
interest, 57
interference, 51
interim progress reports, 56
internal determination, 70
internal motivation, 70
interview(s), 50; with purpose and

intent, 56
invigorate your mission, 20
Israel, 13

James, William, 22
judge your time, 33
judgment rather than
    understanding, 8

key areas in an organization, 37
key leaders, 36, 37, 43
key to learning, 11
keys to taking action, 31
Kimball, Spencer W., 5
kind, 6
kindly persuasion, 101
kindness, 71
kinds of motivations, 59
kinds of planning, 36
knowledge, 4, 26

lack of productivity, 32
lack of accomplishment, 32
lacked social ability, 7
Lao-Tse, 10
law of accomplishment, 82
law of improvement, 82
law of practice, 82
lazy thinker, 92
leader, walks and talks with
    people, 48
leader who thinks, 28
leader's ability, 33
leaders, not born, 1; who really
    care, 6; 25; should be
    prepared, 37; types of, 41;
    who delegate work, 54
leadership, 93, 99, 101
leadership ability, 1, 4, confident
    in, 8; 10, 14
leadership, basic principles of, 5

leadership council, 17, 25, 89
leadership credibility, 5
leadership development, 1
leadership effectiveness, 89
leadership experience, 61
leadership, first basic ingredient
    of, 13
leadership growth process, 1
leadership, power of, 105
leadership processes, 22
leadership skills, 7, 10
leadership team, 19, 30, 43
leadership, three important
    principles of, 2
leadership training meeting, 27
leadership values, 84
leadership vision, 13
learn how to relate and unite, 6
learning, 2; key to, 11; about
    motivation, 60; 102
learning leadership, 1
lecturing, 10
Lee, Harold B., 51
less-active, 39-40
less-productive members, 17
less spiritually advanced people,
    38
less stress, 33
lethargic attitudes, 17
life, basic principle of, 95
lifeless, 7
likeableness, 4
limited and cautious discussion, 8
Lincoln, Abraham, 86
listening, 2; builds confidence, 55
Lord's work, 14
losing team, 85
love, 7; and support, 12; 71
loved by your leaders, 6

magnified light, 25

magnify your calling, 2, 5
magnifying, 5
maintenance problems, 48
major creator, 4
major objectives, 27, 37, 38, 42-
    43, 79
make a difference, 22, 33
making decisions, 8, 29
making quality decisions, 28
managing activities, 25
materialistic enticements, 95
measurable expectations, 20
measurable results, 28, 55
mediocrity, 20; valley of, 29; 41,
    95
mental and physical energy, 28
mental attitude, 6
mental execution, 23
mental exertion, 19, 37, 43
mental fantasizing, 64
mental law, 89
mental pseudo-activity, 64
methods and procedures, 38
methods of reporting, 43
mind is enlightened, 23
minds and hearts of the people, 20
minutes of the meeting, 56, 82, 88,
    89, 92, 93, 107
mission of the Church, 17, 20-21,
    49, 68-69
missionary, 50
mistakes, 54
mixed objectives, 8-9
modify, sharpen, and invigorate
    your vision, 20
momentum to achieve, 37
monitor people performance, 57
monitoring people performance,
    46
monkey theory, 67
moral character, 4, 95

moral principles, 99
moral values, 97
Moses, prepared for his calling, 13; vision concerning his calling, 14; days of, 38
most important objectives, 33
most important principle, 64
most productive members, 17
mother's effectiveness, 54
mothers in training, 54
motivate, 6, or negotiate, 59; 82
motivated person, characteristics of, 61
motivated achievers, 49
motivated leader, 106
motivated people, 67
motivated team, 87
motivated to achieve, 22, 42
motivated to become achievers, 42
motivating climate, 42
motivating knowledge, 26
motivating people in an organization, 60
motivating power, 14, 30, 61
motivating vision statement, 20
motivation, 14, 29; for achievement, 37; 59, 64, 68, 71, 72, 92
motivation, organizational, 68
motivations, and goals, 60; kinds of, 59

need, for planning, 36; first great, 97
needed improvements, 47
needed outcomes, 86
negative, strive to eliminate the, 6; relationship, 59; environment, 70
new and desired outcomes, 22
new callings, 2

new direction, 41, 49
new ideas and new direction, 19
new methods, 37; and ideas, 54
new objectives, 49
new opportunities, 17
new standards of performance, 22
new vision for change, 22
non-defensive leader, 8
nonessential activities, 30
nonjudgmental questions, 10
non-productive conditions, 32, 49
non-thinking leader, 77
normal definition of duty, 5

obedience, 1, 63
obedient followship, 1
obey the Gospel, 23
objective(s), to achieve, 9; and results, 25; 26, to focus on, 33; of the organization, 37-38; 74, 76, 79, 90
observant leader, 57
obstacles, 49
one-on-one debating, 29
open communication, 72
open questions, 17
openness, 6, 12
operational planning, 36-37
operational units, 57
opportunities, 16, 18, 37, 105
opportunity, 1, 5, 32, 51
opposition, 37, of other people, 60
organization, people in the, 15; energy to the, 33; objectives of the, 37; progress of the, 39; results, 49; each unit in the, 57
organization, purpose of, 23, 47, 48, 58, 80
organization, vision of the, 84, 88
organizational analysis, 16
organizational awareness, 48

organizational direction, 20
organizational energy, 25
organizational family, 51
organizational flow, 29
organizational growth, 20
organizational health, 47
organizational improvements, 23
organizational integrity, 89
organizational mediocrity, 41
organizational motivation, 60, 68,
     71, 106
organizational progress, 39
organizational reality, 22
organizational statistics, 47
organizational success, 19
organizational values, 49
organizational vision, 14
organization's performance, 27
organization's success, 35
organize, 8, 74, 76, 77, 79, 80, 91,
     107
organized leader, 35
organizing the areas of focus, 36
other viewpoints, 8
outstanding leadership ability, 4
overall objectives, 38
overall performance, 43
overcome communicating mixed
     objectives, 9
overcome mediocrity, 18, 20

pain of guilt, 97
paper work, 29
participate, and grow, 19
participation, 82
path to greatness, 15
pay the price, 19
people motivation, 60, 65, 71
people improvement, 29
people performance, 57
people problems, 49, 78

perfecting performance, 33
perfection of body and spirit, 5
performance, 82, 88
performance improvement, 29
performing new standards, 22
personal achievement, 64-65
personal goals, 68
personal growth, 1
personal integrity, 97, 103, 107
personal progress, 102
personal recognition, 70
personal vision, 13
personal worthiness, 70
personality, 69
physical problems, 47
physical energy, 28
plan, a blueprint for
     accomplishing, 36; specific
     goals, 38; for success, 42; for
     achieving, 65
planned expectations, 22
planned objectives, 27, 68
planned results, 32, 42
planning, for success, 36; 39;
     passion for, 41; power of, 43,
     106
planning books, 62
planning meetings, 50
point of view, 7, 52
ponder, and think, 19; 24
pondering, 21
poor work performance, 78
position of leadership, 2
positions of responsibility, 21
positive acceptance, 21
positive action, 20
positive attitude, 70
positive climate, 72
positive cycle, 49
positive disposition, 6
positive feelings, 71

positive influence, 61, 100-101, 104
positive information, 69
positive person, 6
positive relationships, 5, 6, 56
positive social ability, 6
possibilities and opportunities, 16
possible hazards, 37
potential, 1, 69
potential concern, 19
potential problems, 7
power in your organization, 33, 42
power of discernment, 61
power of effective operations, 45
power of focusing, 25, 34
power of motivation, 59, 72
power of planning, 35, 43
power of proper example, 67
power of purpose, 15
power of purposeful thinking, 31
power of sustained attention, 28
power of the Holy Spirit, 23
power of vision, 13, 24
power, positions of, 100
power that moves people, 10
power to get things done, 30
power to influence, 4, 26
powerful values, 4
practice self-leadership, 65
practice of writing things down, 63
practice, law of, 82
praise and recognition, 59
prayer, a matter of, 27; 38, 48, 99
praying, 49
pre-determined outcome, 36
precise and meaningful, 7
preparation, 21
prerequisite to analyzing key trends, 39
presentation of expectations, 21

presentations, 31
President Ezra Taft Benson, 38
President Hinckley, 15
President Kimball, 41
President Monson, 2
pressure, 30
price, to pay for growth, 55; for achievement, 65
priesthoods, 5
primary destroyer, 4
primitive impulses, 95
principle of action, 30
principle of effectiveness, 63
principles of leadership, 55
prioritize, 28, 76, 77, 91
priority list, 19, 21
pro-active leader, 35, 47, 88, 93, 106
problem, affects of the, 53
problem conditions, 48
problem solver, 35
problem solving, 48-49, 51-52, 90
problems, 14, 16, 18, 31, 39; two kinds of, 48; dealing with, 54; 84
problems getting along, 50
process for solving, 27
process of learning, 1
procrastinate, 63
procrastination, habit of, 64; 92
product of progress, 48
productive people, 29
productive leaders, 29
productive members, 17
productive working environment, 6
professed values, 4
programs, 25, 78
progress, 8, 51, 56, 86, 90
progress of the organization, 39
progress report, 55-56

progressive leader, 54
promised blessings, 5
promoting activities, 25
prompting of the Spirit, 38
proper example, 17, 68
proper planning, 36
proper recognition, 51
Prophet Joseph Smith, 30
prophets, 38, 95
purpose, 15; and vision, 17; of the
    organization, 20; 38; and
    vision of the organization, 58;
    74, 82; and vision, 84, 106
proposed objectives, 43
purposeful action, focus on, 26;
    30, 33, 105
purposeful ideas, 31
purposeful thinking, 32
putting in time, 17

quality decisions, 28
quick and accurate, 63

reach beyond, 6
reach agreement, 43
reactive leader, 78
reader, 91
reading, 102
reasonable approaches, 55
receiving divine inspiration, 48
receptive, 99
recognition, 51, 59, 104
recognized abilities, 4
reconvert the less active, 15
recorded minutes, 88
recurring positive cycle, 49
reflective questions, 51
relationship with individuals and
    groups, 56
relationships, 50
reliable, 100

renewing of bodies, 5
repentance, 97
reporting, 56
resentment, 55
resourceful leader, 16
resources to achieve, 32
respect, 1-2, 4, 68, 97, 100, 107
respectful obedience, 1
responding to questions, 10
responsibilities, 2, to look ahead,
    14; 51-52, to teach, 54; 55, 97
restitution, 97
result directed, 17, 87
result to be achieved, 54
result-achieving conversation, 8
results, 25, 28, 51, 55, 57, 82, 87,
    92-93, 107
results-oriented leaders, 25
rethink and focus, 27
return and report, 89
returned missionary, struggling, 50
revelation, 60
revised and compelling vision, 18
reward, 28, 106
rewarded, 49
ridged control, 41
right behavior, 100, 104
right decisions, 8
right outcomes, 82
right results, 54
righteous behavior, 99
righteous beliefs, 98
righteous influence, 100, 103, 107
righteous leader, 95; leadership,
    103
righteous principles, 95
risks, 49
rock-solid foundation, 4

sacrament meeting attendance, 39
sanctified by the Spirit, 5

satisfaction, 28
Schwab, Charles, 62
scriptures, read the, 61; teachings of the, 95
secretaries and clerks, 56
seeking agreement, 89
self-discipline, 41
self-effort, 4, 72
self-improvement, 4, 70
self-inspection, 4
self-leadership, 65
self-motivated, leader, 60; person, 61
self-motivation, 60; principle of, 64; 106
self-opposition, 60
self-perfection, 102
self-respect, 97
self, victory over, 60
sense of direction, 15
sense of reliability, 3
sensitive, to people's feelings, 29; 100-101
sensitivity, 71
service, that goes far beyond, 5
service rendered, 61
serving, 5; and leading by example, 12
serving the Lord, 60
set(s) direction, 16, 19, 20, 23
sewer of corruption, 97
shallow, 7
shallow talking, 29
shared agenda, 85
shared information, 70
shared vision, 14-15, 18-20
short-term outcome, 78
showing caring, 12
significant problems, 31
significant results, 2
simplest form of operational

planning, 38
simplify, 91
sincere interest in the people, 21
single purpose, 45
singleness of purpose, 25
skilled leader, 74, 85
skills, 25
smile, 6
Smith, Joseph, 23, 30, 95
Smith, Joseph F., 92
social ability, 2, 5-6, 10, 12, 105
social tranquility, 98
sociality, a very important part of leadership, 5
socializing with the people, 5
soiled, 4
solve problems, 33, 48-49, 58, 90
special council meetings, 17
specific destination, 35
specific goals, 38
specific results, 28, 34, 56
specific revelation, 61
Spirit, in the temple, 60
spirit of enthusiasm, 42
spirit of freedom, 42
spirit of harmony, 71
spirit of love and appreciation, 21
spiritual pain, 97
spiritual power, 60-61
spirituality, 7
spiritually alert, 38
spontaneity, 6
standards of conduct, 99
standards of performance, 28
statical information, 40
statistical information, 47
status quo, 27, 78
sterling qualities, 4
stewardship, 50
still, small voice, 63, 64
stimulated discussion, 17

strategic planning, 36-38
strategic thinker, 37
strengthen your credibility, 11
strengths and weakness, 37
stress, 33, 49, 75, 77
striving to improve, 10
structured times, 51
students, 10
study and prayer, 38
success, 6, 25, 49, 90; guide to, 105
successful achievement, 26, 28
successful leader(s), 35, 87, 88
suffering, 97
sufficient strategic planning, 37
suggestions, 23, 51; for follow up, 56
summarizing conversation, 89
sun rays, 25
superficial answers, 32
superior intelligence, 23
supervision, 59
support his leadership, 66
supportive, 22, 100
supportive relationship, 6
sure concerning decisions, 8
surly disposition, 6
sustained attention, focus on, 26; power of, 28; 30, 33, 105
system thinking, 74
systematize, 74, 77, 79, 80
systemize, 107
systems, power of, 73, 107

talent, 1; and abilities, 59
talking with people, 18
task committees, 92
tasks to achieve, 43
teach, reach, and achieve, 18
teach pertinent principles, 56
teachable, 99

teachers, 10
temple(s), 15, 50, 60; attending the, 61
tendency for shallow talking, 29
tender boldness, 10
test of achievement, 65
thanks and appreciation, 56
thieves, 3
things that matter most, 33
think, analyze, and plan, 19
think and ponder, 19-20, 90
think, plan, and achieve, 41
thinking, to accomplish specific results, 7; 26; and organizing, 29; higher level of, 31; and pondering, 36
thoughts and actions, 4
threats, 37
time managing, 25
time to evaluate, 56
time to ponder and think, 19
timely information, 8
to do items, 62
tobacco, 4
token fulfillment of assignment, 5
tracking method, 79
training and motivation, 67
training meeting, 32
tranquility, 98
trends, 47
trial, error, and study, 59
true credibility, 3
true leadership, 3
trust, 2, climate of, 6; 7, 69, 71, 99
turn on the achieving ability, 11
types of leaders, 41

ultimate objective, 35
uncharted course, 35
unclear expectations, 23
uncomfortable, 6

understanding people's attitudes, 10

understanding, questions to create, 14

unhappy people, 29

united leadership council, 87

unity, level of, 2; 4, 45

unnecessary conversation, 7

unproductive discussions, 29

unselfish objectives, 68

unworthy, 4

up-to-date information, 22

uptight from listening, 7

use your abilities, 33

valley of mediocrity, 29

value in the lives of the people, 20

value of achieving, 22

values, 49, 84, 98-99, 104, 107

veil, 61

very uncomfortable, 6

victory over other men, 10

victory over self, 60

vision, of church work, 15; and clear expectations, 21; a product of diligent prayer, 23

vision and direction, 23

vision of new opportunities, 19

vision of the organization, 13, 15, 58, 84, 88

vision, power of, 24

vision statement, 19-20, 24

vision that requires dedication, 22

visualizing the desired outcome, 37

vital signs, 18-20, 47

voice of the Holy Spirit, 64

walk and talk, 58

weakness, 2; or strength, 29; 99

weaknesses, 18, 37, 61

wealth, 3

welfare, doctrine of, 66, 67

well-being, 71

well-mannered, 6

well-planned systems, 77

willing to learn, 99

willingness to follow, 20

willingness to improve, 64

willingness to listen, 55

wisdom, 61

wise counsel, 8

wishing, 22

without social ability, 6

wonderful feeling, 6

word ability, 3

words of the prophets, 61

work responsibilities, 59

working group, 47

working unit, 46

working with people, 49

worry, 5

worst advice, 5

worthwhile assignments, 50

yearly analysis, 17

yelling, 59